T0299256

"Anyone interested in the art market, either simply as a consumer of art or an investor, should read this book. Especially those who consider art objects as also potential investment tools should find this book particularly useful."

Vito Tanzi, *Honorary President of the International Institute of Public Finance (IIPF), Munich, Germany*

"Andy Warhol famously said: 'Making money is art, and working is art, and good business is the best art'. In this lively book, Andrés Solimano writes about how aesthetics meets money, how this intimate relationship evolved, and what the future holds in turbulent times."

Tony Addison, *Professor, Development Economics Research Group, University of Copenhagen, Denmark*

The Evolution of Contemporary Arts Markets

The Evolution of Contemporary Arts Markets looks at the historical evolution of the art market from the 15th century to the present day. Art is both an expression of human creativity and an object of economic value and financial refuge at times of economic turbulence. Historically, the art market evolved with the development of capitalism, finance and technical change, and art schools responded to social events such as wars, revolutions and waves of democratization.

The author discusses the main features of modern art markets such as complexity in art valuation, globalism, segmentation, financialization, indivisibility, liquidity and provenance issues. The book studies the impact of wealth inequality and economic cycles and crises on the art market and features a chapter focusing specifically on the art market in China.

This accessible publication is ideal for a broad, interdisciplinary audience including those involved in the economic and financial fields as well as art lovers, art market participants and social and cultural scholars.

Andrés Solimano holds a Ph.D in Economics from MIT and is Founder and Chairman of the International Center for Globalization and Development (CIGLOB). He has held senior positions at the World Bank, the Inter-American Development Bank, the Latin American School of Social Sciences (FLACSO) and the United Nations.

Routledge Studies in the Economics of Business and Industry

The Globalisation of Indian Business
Cross border Mergers and Acquisitions in Indian Manufacturing
Beena Saraswathy

Economics and Management in the Biopharmaceutical Industry in the USA
Evolution and Strategic Change
Rachel Kim

Shipbuilding in the United Kingdom
A History of the British Shipbuilders Corporation
Hugh Murphy

Intellectual Property in Russia
Natalia M. Udalova and Anna S. Vlasova

A Market Process Theory of the Firm
An Alternative to the Neoclassical Model
Mateusz Machaj

The Rural Enterprise Economy
Edited by Birgit Leick, Susanne Gretzinger and Teemu Makkonen

The Evolution of Contemporary Arts Markets
Aesthetics, Money and Turbulence
Andrés Solimano

For more information about this series, please visit www.routledge. com/Routledge-Studies-in-the-Economics-of-Business-and-Industry/ book-series/RSEBI

The Evolution of Contemporary Arts Markets
Aesthetics, Money and Turbulence

Andrés Solimano

Routledge
Taylor & Francis Group

LONDON AND NEW YORK

First published 2022
by Routledge
2 Park Square, Milton Park, Abingdon, Oxon OX14 4RN

and by Routledge
605 Third Avenue, New York, NY 10158

*Routledge is an imprint of the Taylor & Francis Group, an
informa business*

© 2022 Andrés Solimano

The right of Andrés Solimano to be identified as author of this
work has been asserted in accordance with sections 77 and 78
of the Copyright, Designs and Patents Act 1988.

All rights reserved. No part of this book may be reprinted
or reproduced or utilised in any form or by any electronic,
mechanical, or other means, now known or hereafter invented,
including photocopying and recording, or in any information
storage or retrieval system, without permission in writing from
the publishers.

Trademark notice: Product or corporate names may be
trademarks or registered trademarks, and are used only for
identification and explanation without intent to infringe.

British Library Cataloguing-in-Publication Data
A catalogue record for this book is available from the British
Library

Library of Congress Cataloging-in-Publication Data
Names: Solimano, Andrés, author. Title: The evolution of
contemporary arts markets : aesthetics, money and
turbulence / Andrés Solimano. Description: Abingdon, Oxon;
New York, NY : Routledge, 2022. | Series: Routledge studies
in the economics of business and industry | Includes
bibliographical references and index. | Contents: The art
market in historical perspective—The art sector in China :
traditional, Maoist and globalized periods—Main features of
the art market : what is art? how to value it? how art trade is
organized?—Recessions, financial crises and war : impact
on the art sector—How the super-rich is shaping the art
sector in an era of high inequality (with Paula Solimano)
Identifiers: LCCN 2021030018 (print) | LCCN 2021030019
(ebook) | ISBN 9781032103938 (hardback) | ISBN
9781032103952 (paperback) | ISBN 9781003215127 (ebook)
Subjects: LCSH: Art—Economic aspects. | Art—Marketing.
Classification: LCC N8600 .S597 2022 (print) | LCC N8600
(ebook) | DDC 381/.457—dc23 LC record available at
https://lccn.loc.gov/2021030018LC ebook record available at
https://lccn.loc.gov/2021030019

ISBN: 978-1-032-10393-8 (hbk)
ISBN: 978-1-032-10395-2 (pbk)
ISBN: 978-1-003-21512-7 (ebk)

DOI: 10.4324/9781003215127

Typeset in Times NR MT Pro
by KnowledgeWorks Global Ltd.

Contents

List of figures   ix
List of tables   x
About the author   xi
Preface   xii
Acknowledgements   xiii

1   Introduction   1

2   The art market in historical perspective   8

2.1   Introduction   8
2.2   The rise of Paris as art centre   9
2.3   Auction houses and American modernism   10
2.4   Art and revolution: Russia (1917) and Mexico (1910)   11
2.5   Muralism, large-scale painting and social transformation   14
2.6   Shifting art centres: The interwar years, WWII and
       American hegemony   16
2.7   Neoliberal capitalism, globalization and the rise of the
       Chinese art market   20

3   The art sector in China: Traditional, Maoist and
    globalized periods   24

3.1   Introduction   24
3.2   Traditional Chinese art   26
3.3   Art and revolution: Maoist China, 1949–1976   29
3.4   The post-Mao period   30
3.5   De-politicizing of society in the 1990s and the boom in
       the art market of the 2000s   33

4 Main features of the art market: What is art?
How to value it? How art trade is organized?   36

4.1 Introduction 36
4.2 Anatomy of the art market 37
4.3 Art according to art critics and art historians 39
4.4 Genius and creativity: View of economists 40
4.5 Special features of the art market 43

5 Recessions, financial crises and war: Impact
on the art sector   56

5.1 Introduction 56
5.2 Crashes and art markets 57
5.3 Sensitivity of art prices to macroeconomic cycles 59
5.4 War and conflict 60

6 How the super-rich is shaping the art sector in an
era of high inequality (with Paula Solimano)   65

6.1 Introduction 65
6.2 The withdrawal of the state in the cultural sector 66
6.3 Hiding art in the shadows: The emergence of freeports 68
6.4 The rise of the super-rich: Wealth
concentration and inequality 69

7 Investing in art as protection against economic
turbulence: Prices in the cycle 1998–2018   74

7.1 Introduction 74
7.2 The 1998 to 2018 period 75
7.3 Is art a safe-haven asset? A comparison
with gold and other assets 79

8 Synthesis and public policy issues   85

References   91
Index   95

Figures

2.1   Global art market share by value in 2018.   23
5.1   The global art market: Value and volume of transactions,
      2008–2018.   60
6.1   Number and wealth of dollar millionaires 2010–2018.   70
6.2   Global share of millionaires wealth more than
      $50 million, 2018.   72
7.1   Quarterly real global prices of art, assets and
      commodities: S&P 500, gold and art price (real prices,
      2015 (Q4) =100, 1998 (Q1) to 2018 (Q4)).   77
7.2   Quarterly real art market prices by country: United
      States, United Kingdom and France (1998 (Q1) – 2018
      (Q2), base 2015 (Q4) = 100, deflated by domestic CPI).   78
7.3   Ratio of the price of gold to stock market prices
      (S&P 500), 1915–2014.   82

Tables

4.1 Share of lots sold and total value at global fine art
auctions in 2017 by price bracket   53
4.2 The art market, the stock market and property markets   55
5.1 The global art market: Value and volume of transactions,
2008–2018   59
6.1 Global share of millionaires (HNWIs), ultra-millionaires
(ultra-HNWIs) and billionaires in total personal wealth
(percent, 2017)   71
7.1 Global real art price index, 1998–2018 (in US$,
base 2015 (Q4) = 100, deflated by US CPI)   76
7.2 Real stock market prices (S&P 500), 1998–2018
(2015 (Q4) = 100, deflated by US CPI)   76
7.3 Real gold prices, 2001–2018 (2015 (Q4) = 100, deflated
by US CPI)   77
7.B.1 Volatility in real prices of art assets and commodities
(fourth quarter of 2004 to second quarter of 2018, real
prices, base 2015 (Q4) = 100)   79
7.4 Real gold price in three slumps (US$ per ounce deflated
by US CPI, ratio peak/trough and percentage change)   80
7.5 Correlation matrix between art prices, financial assets and
commodities (real prices, first quarter of 1998 to second
quarter of 2018)   83

About the author

Andrés Solimano holds a Ph.D in Economics from MIT and is Founder and Chairman of the International Center for Globalization and Development (CIGLOB). He has held senior positions at the World Bank, the Inter-American Development Bank, the Latin American School of Social Sciences (FLACSO) and the United Nations. He holds a PhD in Economics from the Massachusetts Institute of Technology (MIT).

His most recent books as sole author include *The Rise and Fall of the Privatized Pension System in Chile*, Anthem Press (2021), *A History of Big Recessions in the Long 20th Century*, Cambridge University Press (2020) and *Global Capitalism at Disarray, Inequality, Debt and Austerity*, Oxford University Press, 2017. He is also editor of *The International Mobility of Talent: Types, Causes and Development Impact*, Oxford University Press (2008).

He is frequently invited to deliver lectures to main universities and public forums globally.

Preface

This manuscript is the result of research conducted by the author on the intersection of art history, markets, finance, macroeconomics, inequality and social change. Seminars were held at the Investment Migration Council Academic Day 2019 (Geneva, June 3, 2019) and the Inequality and ...? Seminar Series at the European Investment Bank Institute, Luxembourg (June 6, 2019).

Acknowledgements

Comments by Vito Tanzi and collaboration with Paula Solimano in Chapter 6 are greatly appreciated. Effective research assistance conducted by Javier Galaz and Damian Gildemeister on macroeconomic cycles and art prices (Chapter 7) is acknowledged. Kristina Abbotts, Senior Editor at Routledge, provided great support and enthusiasm to the idea of publishing this book. Christiana Mandizha gave effective guidance in the production process.

1 Introduction

Art is a product of human creativity and a means to express inner feelings and beauty. At the same time, art is influenced by its historical context, economic cycles, financial crashes, technological revolutions, financial innovation, political, social and cultural upheavals. In addition, there is also a permanent tension between the dimension of art as aesthetic appreciation open to the citizenship at large (the "masses") through museums and public spaces and art as an investment asset and an object of private collection. Public and private logics to participate in the art sector may vary. In the latter case, the personal availability of wealth and income becomes a critical variable in the ability to acquire and perhaps display art objects to smaller groups with enough purchasing power to acquire them. Art appreciation should be for all, however.

A high volume of liquid capital is circulating around the globe looking for profitable investment opportunities. The art market attracts big money turning artwork a competing asset to stocks, bonds, real estate, gold, foreign exchange and cryptocurrencies. Its current value of global transactions is around 70 billion dollars (c.2019) and rising, benefitting auction houses, galleries, art advisors, financial institutions and, preferably, the most outstanding and well-connected artists.[1]

The definition of artwork comprehends pieces of fine arts such as paintings, sculptures, prints, furniture and decorative arts, antiques and a variety of collectibles. In regard to fine art, a dichotomy has traditionally existed between Modern art (including a variety of movements such as Impressionism, post-Impressionism, Fauvism, Expressionism and Cubism) and Contemporary art, which refers to works created after World War II, and throughout the present. The art market is

1 McAndrew (2019).

DOI: 10.4324/9781003215127-1

notoriously segmented. The sector of small- and medium-size galleries accounts for the bulk of the volume and revenues turnover in the market, while the upper-tier concentrates the high-value transactions but the volume is smaller. In terms of economic impacts, the upper-tier creates only a reduced number of jobs generating high revenues concentrated in a small group of intermediaries.

Art prices can reach really *extravagant* levels and the valuation of art is a very complex topic that we will discuss in this book (chapter 4). It is hard to define the "fundamental value" of an art object. This is in contrast, at least in theory, with the fundamental value of a capital investment (present value of future profits) or real estate (present value of rent payments). However, as highlighted long ago by a main economist of the 20th century, the British John Maynard Keynes, the *future* streams of income associated with a long-lived asset are intrinsically uncertain and thus difficult to anticipate with reasonable precision. Keynes underscored the role of uncertainty on the future that surrounds any exercise of valuation of economic assets, a notion that can be extended also to the valuation of art.

Record prices paid by an artwork are rather common these days in a world with ample liquidity and an elite of very wealthy people. Recently, on March 11, 2021, a digital collage named *Everydays: the first 5,000 days* that collected pieces created every day since May 1, 2007, for 13.5 years, by digital artist Mike Winkelmann – aka Beeple, who is living in North Charleston (South Carolina, USA) – was sold at Christie's for U$69.346 million. This was the first piece of purely digital art sold by the auction house through NFT (non-fungible token that secures authenticity in the blockchain); in turn, the transaction was paid mostly by Ether (the cryptocurrency of Ethereum). The buyer was Singapore-based investor Vignesh Sundaresan – aka Metakovan. *Everydays: the first 5,000 days* was the third most expensive artwork after Jeff Koons and David Hockney. This transaction illustrates the promising marriage between new technologies (the blockchain based on cryptographic techniques) and the art market as the blockchain permits the authentication, say the verification of precedence of artwork.

An absolute record price for an art transaction took place in 2017 when a Leonardo da Vinci painting titled *Salvatore Mundi* sold in New York's Christie's for U$450 million, the highest recorded price ever paid for a work of art (in this case for a dead artist). In turn, in May 2019 the oil canvas *Haystaks* painted in 1890 by Claude Monet was sold at an auction in Sotheby's at U$110 million (the pre-sale valuation was at U$50 million).[2] In the same month at Christie's Jeff Koons sold the stainless steel *Rabbit* for U$91 million, setting a record price for work by a living artist. In addition, David Hockney's *Portrait of an Artist: A Pool with Two Figures* was sold for U$90.3 million. On other occasions, pieces of Modern art (Van Gogh, Klimt, Kandinsky, Monet, Leger and Chagall) have sold in the price range of U$11 to U$80 million, and those by top Postwar and Contemporary artists, such as Andy Warhol, Jean-Michel Basquiat, Roy Lichtenstein, Mark Rothko, Gerhard Richter and Cy Twombly, the range of U$20 million–U$110 million (McAndrew, 2018). It is apparent that these extravagant prices make fashionable artwork only affordable to a minuscule portion of the global population with very large wealth, stressing the elitist nature of the upper-end of the art market. An implication of this is that public museums also face hard times to expand their collections due to the rising price of valuable artwork at a time of tighter acquisitions budgets.

There are multiple motivations for acquiring art. It can be considered as a "consumption good" driven by aesthetic enjoyment and the quest for objects that capture beauty. In addition, art is also a "symbolic asset" with features of conspicuous consumption (Thorsten Veblen's famous term) in which owners of highly valuable artwork use it to signal their command of high wealth.[3] On the other hand, the demand for artwork is also motivated by the expectation of a monetary return associated with an increase (appreciation) in its price. In this case, art becomes an investment asset in which return-risk combinations compared to other assets become very relevant considerations. More prosaic motivations for investing in art may also include practices of money laundering and tax avoidance by individuals and organizations engaged in drug traffic and illegal arms trade, taking advantage of the unregulated character of the art market. The loss of tax revenues associated with unrecorded art transactions deprives government of revenues that could be used to support promising artists, public museums and public exhibitions contributing to both the production of art and the social welfare through the enjoyment of art.

Art does not proceed in an absolute vacuum. Historical events, economic crises, wars, revolutions, cycles of democratization and

---

2 The sale price of this painting in 1986 was U$2.5 million, increasing by 44 times in a period of 33 years.

3 Mandel (2009) discusses the investment and consumption features of artwork.

authoritarianism, social upheavals all affect the process of artistic creation and spur new art movements. Muralism, for example, was triggered by the Mexican revolution of 1910 and its aftermath with the Mexican government actively supporting muralism in the decades after the revolution. However, muralism was not only circumscribed to Mexico. In Spain, Pablo Picasso depicted some of the horrors of the Spanish civil war in his large-scale *Guernica* painting. In turn, the Chilean surrealist-muralist Roberto Matta, who was living in Europe, on a working trip to Chile in 1971, along with the Ramona Parra (painting) Brigade made murals in street walls located in popular neighbours, during the processes of progressive social transformation undergoing in Chile under the government of president Salvador Allende.

In turn, after the Bolshevik revolution in Russia, there was an outburst of artistic creativity around artists such as Malevich, Popova, Chagall, Kandinsky and others that followed constructivism, futurism, minimalism. This art current also reached design and architecture. This movement, however, faded away after the onset of Stalinism and socialist realism that restricted freedom of artistic expression.

After World War I flourished the tendencies of Surrealism, Dadaism and other forms of abstract art and after World War II, Abstract Expressionism developed with force. In China during the rule of Mao Tse Tung's (1949–1976), art was predominantly viewed as an active political tool (along the lines of soviet socialist realism under Stalin), but this trend was eventually repelled as the country moved in the 1980s and 1990s to marketization and globalization although limitations persisted for the development of independent and dissident art.

Economic globalization and the expansion of international financial markets boosted also the globalization of the art market and the influence of finance and new technologies in the trading of artwork. It is clear that economic and technological change leads to changes in the market for art objects.

Twenty-first global capitalism is constantly reproducing and expanding the wealth held by rich elites and highly rewarded individuals in the financial and other sectors that accumulate assets and receive large income flows. These prosperous segments need to find new outlets for investing their wealth. Thus, art becomes an attractive alternative to invest and diversify portfolios albeit with some potential complications.[4] The affluence of the economic elites exerts direct

---

4 See Solimano (2014, 2017) for analysis of elites, wealth distribution and global capitalism.

influence over the art industry through at least two channels: (i) the purchase of art making many pieces unaffordable to potential buyers from the middle and working classes and (ii) a growing influence over the policies of museums and cultural organizations through their presence in board of directors of museums following the declining public support for the arts.

In the age of neoliberalism, we observe a trend towards the *commodification and financialization* of the art sector. The rising importance of private money is leading to increased *segmentation and centralization* of sales in big auction houses and large galleries. Collusive practices regarding minimum prices, commissions, cosy links between sellers, buyers and intermediaries are not uncommon.

Furthermore, there is an active market for stolen, forged and faked artwork whose annual sales are estimated in the range of U$6 to U$10 billion. In general, no more than 5 percent of stolen art is recovered as prosecution of these practices is not a high priority for governments around the world. As a consequence of this, the transaction costs of buying and selling artwork in the formal market increase due to the need to verify the provenance of pieces traded.

Another relevant issue is the impact on the art market of macroeconomic cycles and financial crises at national and international levels. The main global economic cycles of the last 100 years include the great depression of the 1930s, the stagflation of the 1970s, the global financial crisis of 2008–2009 and the 2020–2021 pandemics. A related question in financial analysis is to gauge to what extent artwork constitutes a "safe-haven" asset, protecting the wealth of investors in a world of substantial financial volatility and frequent economic crises. The book presents historical and recent evidence on the behaviour of art prices compared to competing assets during the various episodes of economic and financial crises ending with an analysis of the period 1998–2018 as well as reviews the impact of World War I and World War II on the French and Belgium art markets in Europe.

This book is organized into eight chapters including this introduction. Chapter 2 provides a historical overview of the art market since the 15th century to the present, documenting the evolutionary nature of the art sector, the rise and fall of main geographical art centres and the appearance and demise of new conceptual currents following revolutions, wars and other epochal changes. Chapter 3 examines main trends in Chinese art from imperial times through the 20th century and early 21st century. Traditional Chinese art included ink-painting, watercolours and gouaches that depicted mountains, rivers, court members and conveyed intellectual and religious messages. The influence of Western art and Japanese art was important between 1911 and 1949 with a sharp decline in the Maoist period when art was viewed mainly as a tool of political mobilization a trend that exacerbated during the years of the Cultural Revolution (1966–1976). As China moved to markets, globalization and tolerated higher internal economic inequality, the art sector also underwent important transformations. Artists started to criticize the political control of the party and the state and the type of art in favour during the Maoist period. Aesthetic motives in the post-Mao era included a more personal search of meanings, abstractionism and new conceptual art. In turn, in the 1990s and 2000s, main international auction houses such as Christie's and Sotheby's opened operations in mainland China. A class of new riches became collectors interested in buying western and local art and foreign buyers became interested in collecting Chinese art. In the 2010s, the Chinese market consolidated into second/third place in terms of global sales after the United States alternating the second place with the United Kingdom (see Chapter 6).

Chapter 4 addresses main conceptual and empirical features of art markets regarding how to do the valuation of artwork, the heterogeneity of products in the art sector, transaction costs, liquidity and the impact of new blockchain technologies. The chapter also stresses the sensitivity of the art market's sales and prices to overall macroeconomic and financial cycles, the impact of wealth inequality on the art market, its segmentation and concentration and its growing internationalization and geographical concentration in the United States, United Kingdom and Chinese markets that, combined, account for near 80 percent of global sales, displacing the previous importance of France, Germany and Japan as main trading places for artwork. Chapter 5 presents historical cases of recessions, financial crashes and war in terms of their impact on the art market. The chapter reviews empirical evidence comparing the return of holding art and financial assets (equities, bonds) and gold during World War I and World War II in France and Belgium examining the impact of inflation, financial repression and monetary reform on investments in art. Chapter 6 examines the conceptual and empirical connections between wealth inequality, economic elites and the art market and how the growing concentration of wealth in small elites has been pushing up art prices, particularly in the upper segment of the market. The chapter also explores the role of freeports and other mechanisms of tax reduction on the art sector. Chapter 7 studies the behaviour of art prices in the cycle 1998–2018, a period that includes boom, crash (2008–2009), stagnation and erratic recoveries.

The evolution of art prices during cycles is compared also with stock market prices, gold prices, oil prices and bitcoin prices. Chapter 8 discusses the main conclusions of the book and highlights basic public policy issues regarding support for artists, autonomy of small and middle size galleries, dominance of large galleries, and preservation of cultural heritage in the art sector.

2 The art market in historical perspective

2.1 Introduction

The art market developed in an evolutionary way starting in the Renaissance in the 14th–15th centuries. It followed the commercial actions of merchants and dealers that obtained in estate sales furniture, carpets, porcelains, sculptures, paintings, printings, engravings. Part of the artworks was done by independent artists and craftsmen. They were often commissioned for decoration of *palazzos* (mansions), public offices, churches and cathedrals by kings, the church and wealthy families. An important distinction is between primary markets (production and first-sale) and secondary markets (of resale and collection). In the primary market segment, the sales are often conducted by the artists themselves while the secondary market is linked to the action of art dealers, artist's agents and, later, the auction houses. In France, in the mid-16th century, a state monopoly for auctioning artwork was granted and this institution survived for five centuries until 2001.[1]

In the second half of the 15th century, Florence became the main centre of finance, commerce and concentration of painters and sculptors; truly an epicentre of the Renaissance era in finance, manufacturing, art and various cultural manifestations. The Medici family, who ruled Florence, was an important patron of artists. In northern Europe, by the end of the 15th century, the city of Bruges started as an important city for art trade and commerce with a flourishing community of merchants and artisans. Bruges was more a multinational centre of art trade while Florence was a local and regional market.

1 Renda (2015) and De Marchi and Van Maegroti (2006).

DOI: 10.4324/9781003215127-2

In Bruges, three guilds of artists were important: oil painters, water-colour painters and miniaturists. They displayed their works in the *pands* that were large public markets in which art objects were shown in courtyards and shop windows. Antwerp later also started to compete with Bruges in art and benefitted from its significant role in international trade. Later, between the 16th and 18th centuries, Venice, Amsterdam and Rome also played significant roles in the trading of paintings, sculptures, printing and engraving. The involvement of main cities was beneficial for the development of the secondary market with an increasingly important role played by the art dealer and auction houses.

Second-hand dealers in estate sales trading in cloth and artwork were known as *riggatieri* in Italy, rag and bone men in Britain, *fripiers* in France and *oudecleerkopers* in Holland.[2] Specialization developed, and a segment of these dealers specialized in art objects became engaged in auctions giving rise to a thicker and sophisticated market for art. Systems of quality guarantees and oversight of the provenance of paintings and other artefacts were gradually introduced in the high end of the market. Amsterdam, Rome and then London with their networks of dealers and auction houses become important centres for the trading of art.

2.2 The rise of Paris as art centre

In the first half of the 18th century, Paris started to gain importance as an art centre. The dealer Edme-Francois Gersaint invented methods for attracting participants to auctions, using printed catalogues before exhibitions and catered prospective buyers to develop an appreciation for artwork.

The state-led auction house at the hotel Drouot, located near the Paris stock exchange, was opened in 1850. There are two main auctioning traditions: the English system and the Dutch system. In the former, an auction starts at a low price and rises during the auction until a "hammer price" is reached. In contrast, in the Dutch system, the auction starts at the highest price and goes down in descending order of prices throughout the auction.

The "Paris Salon", the state-sponsored official exhibit of the French Academy of Fine Arts was the main judge of what could be considered as "accepted art", setting standards that guided art markets, at

2 Renda (2015).

least for a while. The Salon was rather conservative and excluded more innovative and iconoclast artists. This was the case, for example, of the Impressionist school – Monet, Manet, Cezanne, Pissarro, Degas and others – that had to find new venues for showing their work after being rejected by the official Paris salons.

The French art dealer Paul Durand-Ruel was instrumental in promoting the impressionists, post-impressionists, Fauvists (Matisse, Derain and others) and avant-garde schools that were making strides in the late 19th and early 20th centuries. Durand-Ruel also had connection with the London art market and contributed to internationalizing French artists.[3]

Another important art dealer that contributed to bringing European art to the United States at the turn of the 20th century was Sir Joseph Duveen, partner of the Duveen Brothers firm based in London with branches in New York and Paris. Duveen's genius was his appreciation of the potential of the North American art market guided by the notion that "Europe has a great deal of art and America has a great deal of money". The gilded age and new fortunes made in America by Du Pont, Rockefeller, Carnegie, Stanford and other wealthy individuals were important in the founding of art museums, the creation of universities, the general promotion of culture and the patronizing of art. Duveen was very successful in cultivating wealthy American individuals as his main clients. In addition, Duveen had accumulated a great fortune himself dealing with art and formed an important collection of his own, making also significant donations to British art museums, contributing to boost the art sector in Britain.[4]

2.3 Auction houses and American modernism

The two main auction houses we have today in the world: Sotheby's and Christie's are both of British origin. Sotheby's was established in 1744 and specialized for near two centuries in rare books – they sold

---

3 Galenson (2009) traces the development of the modern art market in the early parts of the 20th century as following the end of the monopoly of who and which type of art style could exhibit their work in Paris's grand salons exerted by the government-sponsored Society of Fine Arts. Claude Monet and a group of impressionists challenged in the 1870s this monopoly and set-up the Salon des Independents, allowing for more pluralism and the emergence of an array of independent art dealers in the late 19th century and early 20th century.
4 Secrest (2005).

a copy of Dante Alighieri's *Divina Commedia* illustrated by Sandro Botticelli – before turning into art auctions in the mid-1940s. Christie's was founded in 1766 having as its main focus the art world. Since the 1950s these auction houses opened offices in several countries in North America, Europe and Asia contributing to the gradual globalization of the art market. A third, much more recent art auction housing that tried to break the Sotheby's-Christie's duopoly was Phillips de Pury & Company founded in 2002.

In the second half of the 19th century, European, particularly French art dominated the western scene, and this influenced the US market. At the turn of the 20th century, a new impulse came from the American art sector that saw the emergence of two schools: the "ashcan school" and the "modernists". The former focussed on social realism depicting poverty and slumps in American cities. Representatives of the social realism were George Luks, John Sloan and Everett Shinn. The modernists, in turn, were more influenced by European art trends such as Impressionism, Fauvism and Cubism. An event known as "the group of eight" presented work of these two schools at the Macbeth Gallery in New York city followed by the Armory Show of 1913 organized by Alfred Stieglitz. This event brought Picasso, Matisse and Duchamp to America and it was an impulse for renewal of art in North America under the label of "American Modernism". This included a diversity of artists such as Georgia O'Keeffe and a group of non-figurative and abstract American artists such as Max Weber, John Marin, Arthur Dove, Marsden Hartley, Abraham Walkowitz and Arthur B. Carles. This group found a place to show their work in the Newark Museum, the Phillips Collection and the new Whitney Museum located in New York City.

Art is influenced by political developments and social phenomena. World War I had an impact on art created in the search for meaning in human life shattered by a highly destructive conflict of international proportions. The development of Cubism, Minimalism, Abstract art, Constructivism and other trends in the early decades of the 20th century, no doubt, were shaped by the mix of conflict, despair and also the hopes for benign social change.

2.4 Art and revolution: Russia (1917) and Mexico (1910)

The collapse of the Czarist regime in Russia in February of 1917 and the October revolution led by the Bolsheviks entertained the promise of liberation from imperial traditions and gave rise to hopes of a socialist future of equality. This unleashed a period of strong artistic creativity by the "Russian avant-garde" that lasted until the late 1920s before being suppressed by the emergence of socialist realism as official art and the consolidation of Stalinism and the bureaucratization of Soviet society. The avant-garde in its early origins was, in general, hostile to "traditional academic art". In 1863, a group of artists that embraced this movement left the Imperial Academy of Art in Saint Petersburg. The two best-known artists (in the west) of the Russian avant-garde were Marc Chagall and Wassily Kandinsky. Both, eventually, left Russia and settled in Europe in the 1920s. Chagall was initially an active participant in the Russian revolution. He was named art commissary for the Vitebsk region where he founded the Vitebsk art school in 1919. However, the bureaucratic burdens of the directorship position and controversies with Kazimir Malevich were too much for Chagall. Malevich was the leader of the supremacist movement geared to the achievement of a utopian future through merging geometric forms and artistic feelings.[5] These tensions urged Chagall to abandon the Vitebsk school moving to Moscow in 1920 and then leaving Russia to Paris in 1923.[6] Constructivism was perhaps more practically oriented than the supremacist and expressed themselves through posters, sculpture and architecture. Two important figures in the constructivist movement were Alexander Rodchenko and Liubov Popova.[7] These artists believed that art had to play an active social function and not only a decorative role. They wanted art to reach the masses, energized by the prospect of a different future from the one associated with Czarist rule, and not only serve as objects of contemplation for wealthy elites. In its architectural bent, the movement provided housing solutions to the people also an objective of the Bolshevik revolution. Moscow's Narkomfin building was a clear example of community living that included a kindergarten and a canteen, a place oriented to freeing women from domestic tasks and thus allowing the female to work in industry, agriculture, government activities and services within the general notion that women had to be incorporated to different tasks of building a new society.

The avant-garde also introduced important innovations in fashion, clothing and design. The latter included the design of buildings, factories and transportation systems. El Lissitzky, a disciple of Malevich, was an important figure in the Russian abstract movement including

5 State Russian Museum (2000).
6 Russian Avant Garde (1981).
7 Sarabianov and Adaskina (1990).

suprematism and constructivism. He was a member of the UNOVIS group (makers of the new art), had been invited by Chagall to join the Vitebsk school. This Russian artist later became an influence on the Bauhaus school.

Artistic experimentation was an overriding feature of the Russian avant-garde in the period 1920–1925 and the group was also known as "artists of the left". New currents included futurism, productivism, symbolism, concretism and "engineerism". These branches were far from coherent among them and feuds and divisions were common. As the art critic Harold Rosenberg observed: "Each avant-garde movement is always on the verge of going to war with itself".[8]

Eventually, the Russian avant-garde artists and their production went into virtual hiding under Stalin that in the cultural realm was imposing "socialism realism", say using art for soviet propaganda directly depicting factories, heroic workers meeting five-year plan targets, sports heroes, victory at second world war and so on. In this cultural climate, the output of abstract artist's work, which had been very prolific in the early 1920s, would not be acquired by official museums and galleries. As a sign of the times "public" exhibitions were presented in semi-clandestine ways many times outside urban centres literally in the woods in the 1960s and 1970s.

Consequently, the art market for avant-garde failed to develop in a closed society that had banished free and independent thinking. However, there were still a few collectors of abstract Russian art in the 1940s, 1950s, 1960s and 1970s. A remarkable case was George Costakis, a Russian citizen born in Greece, who was living in the Soviet Union, working at the Greek embassy. Over the decades Costakis managed to form a private collection of more than 2,500 artworks produced by Kandinsky, Chagall, Popova, Tatlin, Malevich and Rodchenko. The avant-garde artworks were often acquired by Costakis at very low prices since this was considered as unofficial and dissident art, therefore carrying the risks of selling and buying these pieces. In the 1970s, part of the Costakis collection was donated to the Tretyakov Gallery in Moscow.

Another social uprising spurring a period of artistic creativity was the Mexican revolution of 1910. It inspired the Mexican muralist movement that flourished in the 1920s and 1930s. The Mexican revolution, not exempted of violence mainly in the 1910s, was a tumultuous process of economic, social and cultural transformation that unleashed

8 Rosenberg (1967).

a far-reaching process of social and cultural change. Eventually, the revolution became "institutionalized" in the 1940s and 1950s losing its fresh energy and turned far more conservative and rigid.

2.5 Muralism, large-scale painting and social transformation

The three main exponents of the muralist movement were Diego Rivera, Jose Clemente Orozco and David Alfaro Siqueiros. Nonetheless, the Mexican artistic milieu included also other names such as Frida Kahlo, Francisco Goitia and others. Murals typically depicted different periods of Mexican history. They presented the pre-Columbian roots of Aztec and Mayan civilizations, the process of independence from Spain and denounced American and French interventions in the 19th century. The murals often exalted the revolution of 1910 and the role of peasants, workers and oppressed groups in Mexican history. They were very colourful and displayed magnificent designs of pyramids and temples. In the 1920s, the Mexican government commissioned murals for public buildings such as the presidential palace in Mexico-city, for universities, schools and public places in the idea of making art accessible to the rank and file of society and not only to small elites.

Muralists also reached outside Mexico. Rivera made inroads into the United States and painted a mural named "Detroit Industry" for Ford Motor Company in Detroit in 1932–1933. This work illustrated the capitalist factory system for automobiles and its impact on the shop-floor workers and society at large. Another commission of Rivera was less successful. This was the case of the mural "Man at the Crossroads Looking with Hope and High Vision to the Choosing of a New and Better Future" which was two-thirds complete at the time that was forced to be removed from the Rockefeller Center in New York City. The main reason for the removal was that the mural included depictions of Vladimir Ilyich Lenin, the most important leader of the Bolshevik revolution, and contained openly left-wing content deemed inappropriate for a Center located on New York's fifth avenue, an epicentre of American capitalism. This episode marked the start of the decline of Rivera's clout with patrons in the United States. Nonetheless, Orozco managed to paint a mural at the New School of Social Research in New York City, a piece that remains until today.

Muralism does not only pertain to Mexican artists. As mentioned before, a main mural, "Guernica" was painted in the 1937 by Spanish painter Pablo Picasso. It depicted in surreal fashion the bombing of the small city of Guernica that was the capital of the Basque country by joint nationalist art force supporting general Francisco Franco and German warplanes under the orders of Adolf Hitler. Picasso reflected in a large canvas the destruction and drama of that bombing to a city that was not a military target.

In South America, social revolutions in the second half of the 20th century also were accompanied by an outburst of muralism. In Bolivia, the revolution of 1952 led by Victor Paz Estenssoro and his Movimiento Nacional Revolucionario (National Revolutionary Movement) nationalized tin mines and oil facilities and launched a process of agrarian reform to distribute land to the peasantry. The new regime promoted muralism to display the themes of progressive social transformation and educate the masses. Leading muralists were Walter Solon Romero, Miguel Alandia Pantoja, Lorgio Vaca and Gil Imana Pantoja. In 1953, Alandia Pantoja finished the mural *History of the Mine* and in 1956 five murals were painted on the building of the state-owned oil company YPFB. One theme was "El Petroleo Boliviano" (The Bolivian Oil). Decades later, in 1980, these murals were destroyed in a military coup led by right-wing dictator Luis Garcia Meza.

In Chile, between 1970 and 1973 during the presidency of Salvador Allende's and its "Chilean way to socialism" pursued peacefully and within the legal framework existing in the country at the time, public murals painted on walls, streets and walled river's borders were used as a creative propaganda tool by the Brigadas Ramona Parra (BRP) associated with the youth of the Chilean Communist Party. The BRP's artistic expressions were inspired by previous muralism from Mexican and Spanish origins. An important mural that was buried under a thick coat of wall painting, for many years during the military regime of General Pinochet was "El Primer Gol de Chile (the first goal of the Chilean people)" painted by the Chilean surrealist artist Roberto Matta in his 1971 visit to Chile along with the Brigade Ramona Parra. This was a fresco of 24 × 5 meters, that is currently displayed in the *Centro Cultural Espacio Matta* located in the popular neighbourhood of La Granja in the capital city of Santiago.

Returning to Mexico, Frida Kahlo, the wife of Diego Rivera, not a muralist herself, was an important Mexican surrealist painter. Surrealist champion Andre Breton promoted Frida and helped to organize an exhibition for her in Paris in late 1939. Earlier that year, Breton had written the catalogue essay for a Frida show at the Julien Levy Gallery in New York City. Feminist and post-modernist themes were important in Kahlo's work besides other personal and socio-political motivations.

International artists such as photographers were attracted to the Mexican socio-political and cultural scene and the vital and energetic art movement that it had triggered. This included Tina Modotti (also an activist) from Italy, the French Henri Cartier-Bresson, Paul Strand and the Hungarian Frank Cappa (Endre Erno Friedmann) to cite the most famous. In the second half of the 20th century, the muralist movement eventually faded away coinciding with the turn to one-party rule in Mexico led by the Partido Revolucionario Institucional (PRI) since the 1940s. Canvases were preferred to walls. The famous painter Rufino Tamayo switched to fruits, vegetables and life in popular fresh markets as the main motives of his paintings.

2.6 Shifting art centres: The interwar years, WWII and American hegemony

From the mid-19th century to the early decades of the 20th century the British and French markets were dominant in the art world. Paris remained an important art centre in the interwar period and left bank galleries flourished in the secondary market for Impressionism, post-Impressionism, Cubism, Fauvism and other genres. An important school of visual art including painting, drawing, collage, photography, sculpture, film-making developed in Paris headed by Andre Breton and aimed at exploring the irrational (supra-real), unsettling and dreamy aspects of surroundings and the mind. Main figures of the surrealist movement were filmmaker Luis Buñuel (Spanish), Salvador Dali (Spanish), Max Ernest (German), Joan Miro (Spanish), Man Ray (American), Roberto Matta (Chilean), Kurt Seligman (Swiss) and Yves Tanguy (French). Women surrealists artists include Leonora Carrington (UK), Frida Kahlo (Mexican), Remedios Varo (Spain) and Marcia Martins (Brazilian).

The work of surrealist artists was influenced by the desire to find ways to express inner feelings and take stances in a world in disarray and confusion emerging from the "great war" in 1914–1917 and its shaky aftermath. The surrealist, at a conceptual level, were also impelled by the psychoanalytic theories of Sigmund Freud.[9]

The economic environment of a country certainly influences the art market. The "roaring 1920s" (economically speaking) in the United States entailed in the first half of the decade an economic boom in the real estate market (Florida and others) followed by a boom in the stock market in the second half until the stock market crash of 1929. In the early 1930s, the previous boom was reversed giving to "the

---

9 Important art critics in the United States that studied and supported abstract expressionism were Harold Rosenberg and Clement Greenberg.

great depression" in the United States and a score of countries in what turned out to be the worst crisis that experienced the global capitalist system in the 20th century (Solimano, 2020).

In America, a consortium of art dealers, short of money due to the economic depression, sold an important collection of masterpieces to the industrialist Andrew Mellon and this formed the basis of the National Gallery of Art established in Washington, DC. In retrospect, the 1930s and 1940s were favourable decades for the large art public museums in the United States and they became main patrons for artists, more important than the private sector. In turn, Harvard University started offering courses on museum studies.

An important program of government support for the art in the 1930s was the Federal Art Project (FAP), part of the broader Works Progress Administration (WPA). The FAP subsidized local artists to paint canvases, murals, posters and make decorations in public buildings. In those days, the American State promoted artists in an active way. One of the artists that received these subsidies was Jackson Pollock who was trained in new muralist techniques taught by the Mexican artists Jose Clemente Orozco and David Alfredo Siqueiros. Pollock also attended workshops on surrealist art offered by Roberto Matta at that time residing in New York.

The Mexicans introduced Pollock in 1936 (at the age of twenty-four) into spray paint, paint-gun techniques, synthetic resins such as Duco and acrylic paint as the medium. Later, Pollock would use these new techniques for his "drip painting" in the 1940s that drove him to fame paving the way as a top representative of "abstract expressionism". Pollock, however, had a jumbled private life, was into alcoholism and died in 1956 in an accident when the car he was driving crashed against a tree.

Since World War II, the United States became the global hegemonic power in both economic and military terms. At the same time, the United States of America started to gain global importance in the art world with New York City becoming a main centre of attraction for the residence of foreign (mainly European) artists and the commercialization of art objects. In fact, New York started to displace Paris as a main centre art market in the world, attracting top European artists that were looking for a peaceful (at least compared to interwar Europe) and prosperous environment to develop their art.

In fact, the rise of fascism and Nazism in the 1930s and then the outbreak of World War II in the early 1940s prompted the flying to the United States of main painters such as Roberto Matta, Max Ernst, Yves Tanguy and others. Also, several art dealers moved from Europe to America, mainly to New York, in the 1930s and 1940s.

In retrospect, World War II and the ensuing reconfiguration of global power that followed it prompted the shifting of the geographic core of the global art sector towards America (New York) as it prompted a flight of artists from Europe to America which had no war in its territory and that was a country of growing material prosperity. Another (perhaps unexpected) effect of the war was that in occupied countries such as France, Belgium and the Netherlands the occupation by the Nazis boosted the demand for artwork as a safe asset, leading to the rise of art prices (see Chapter 5), something that did not occur in World War I. This was a consequence of at least two factors: (i) the high purchasing power of German occupants that were keen to acquire art collections and (ii) the high liquidity of the "nouveaux riches" formed by black marketeers and shopkeepers that made big profits selling necessities in a shortage economy. The "nouveaux riches" were interested in investing in art given its features of discretion, portability and protection against inflation and "financial repression".

The looting of art collections of rich Jew families in Germany and Europe also brought to the market for sale objects that before were held in private homes. Jewish art dealers and galleries were also targeted. Meanwhile, the cultural policy of Nazi Germany was openly hostile to "degenerate art" , as called by the Nazis, of modern art such as abstractionism, Dadaism, cubism, futurism that had flourished in the interwar period and before. This included work by Matisse, Modigliani, Van Gogh, Kandinsky and others that were banned from exhibition and confiscated in German museums and public collections. Confiscated artwork that was considered "degenerate" was either destroyed or shipped to Switzerland and other countries for sale.

When the Germans occupied Paris, the *Jeu de Paume* museum at the Tuileries Garden was transformed into a central collection point receiving most looted art brought from different parts of France. Confiscated objects were there registered and classified. A main role in the art policy of Nazi Germany was played by Hermann Goering, who was obsessed with art collection and visited several times the museum *Jeu de Paume*. Other high-level Nazi officials as Rosenberg and Von Ribbentrop also participated in this policy of the Third Reich. An exception in the predominant policy of looting was Count Wolff Metternich, of the German army in occupied France, who initially adopted a policy of safeguard of valuable art following the guidelines of the 1907 Hague convention on war. Eventually, he had to concede to the wishes of the more powerful, higher-level officials. Many works were repatriated to Germany and sent to the private collections of Nazi officials and to museums. Received paintings by Picasso,

Picabia, Ernst, Arp, Dali, Miro and Leger were just destroyed and had to be subtracted from the world heritage of the fine arts.[10] On the fiscal-financial side, the need to finance the war and occupation expenses also indirectly affected the art market. Techniques of "financial repression" were oriented to encourage the acquisition of government bonds by individuals and firms. These bonds when subscribed provided money to the public treasury to finance public expenditure associated with war. The fiscal deficit could be also covered by printing money by central banks in exchange for government bonds. Governments also could increase taxation – not a very popular expedient in wartime – or get foreign loans. In order to induce the acquisition of public bonds, a policy of squeezing the financial return of holding equity (stocks issued by private corporations) was pursued through special registration procedures and caps on price increases. Under these conditions, wealth holders and people with excess liquidity turned to the art market that offered discretion, portability and price appreciation.

Returning to the interactions between local and exiled artists, the exiled European artists residing on US soil such as Roberto Matta and others met with surrealists such as Arshile Gorky (of Armenian origin), Mark Rothko (born in Russia), Jackson Pollock, Willem de Kooning (from the Netherlands) and Robert Motherwell. These exchanges were very important in the development of abstract expressionism in the 1940s and 1950s. This could be the first artistic movement that shifted the centre of Western art from Europe to the United States, particularly to New York City. Abstract expressionism made innovative use by individuals of new synthetic industrial paints, large-scale canvases and abstract styles. For example, Rothko's use of large blocks of colour, the drips and splatters of Jackson Pollock and Franz Kline's quick and simple brushstrokes.

It is argued that abstract expressionism was used also as a sort of cultural weapon in the cold war, with the MOMA (Museum of Modern Art in New York) and perhaps the Central Intelligence Agency (CIA) playing roles in exporting new American art to Europe in the late 1950s and presenting it as a more free spirit/style, iconoclast alternative that emerged in open societies in contrast to the formulaic propaganda of "socialist realism" of the USSR.

Another trend that shaped the art world in the second half of the 20th century in North America and Europe was the internationalization of auction houses along with the growth of the secondary art market

10 Oosterlinck, K. (2011) and Feliciano, H. (1995).

a process in which contributed art dealers such as Leo Castelli in the United States, wealthy collectors such as Peggy Guggenheim and others.

2.7 Neoliberal capitalism, globalization and the rise of the Chinese art market

In the period spanning from early 1950 to the early 1970s, advanced economies lived a period of managed capitalism – the so-called "golden age of capitalism" – characterized by rapid growth, high investment, employment security, a degree of labour-capital cooperation and the absence of large-scale financial crises in advanced economies. This was a period of material prosperity and reasonable social peace although this phase should not be romanticized if we consider that the "cold war" between the United States of America and the USSR induced in America anti-communist witch-hunting (McCarthyism) affecting the cultural sector in that country (extending to radio, TV and Hollywood). Artists were also harassed during the anti-communist wave that affected America in the 1950s.

In the 1970s and early 1980s, as a consequence of the fiscal and monetary contradictions that managed capitalism entertained the system suffered from inflation, exchange rate instability, lack of productivity growth and fiscal difficulties. As a response to these maladies, the United States of America and the United Kingdom along with Pinochet's Chile in the third world applied policies of marketization, labour repression and privatization, entering into a "neoliberal phase" of capitalism still prevailing now. Neoliberal capitalism relies, at least at a rhetorical level, more strongly on markets than the golden age and financial capital becomes internationally mobile in the search for new profit opportunities. The neoliberal model redistributes income and wealth to economic elites, which become more powerful and influential. At the same time, the labour unions and civil society organizations are weakened to ensure an unchallenged rule of capital. In the cultural sector, art becomes commodified and financialized following a dominant capitalist logic of profit orientation (see Chapter 4).[11]

The transition from managed capitalism to neoliberal capitalism has had several effects on the art sector that can be summarized as follows:[12]

i Growing influence of private finance on the art market as a trend also affecting public museums, art fairs and cultural publications.

---

11 Solimano (2014) and McAndrew (2018).
12 See Solimano and Solimano (2020).

ii Increasing links between international and national economic elites and the art market through the private purchase of highly valuable artworks, the creation of high-end art galleries, the boosting of large, internationalized, auction houses as a main vehicle to sell art. This is complemented by the growing role of international art fairs catered to rich art buyers.

iii The increasing use of the art market for financial diversification of the portfolios of professional investors and individual wealth-owners. Art objects are increasingly used as a refuge to face the volatility of financial markets affected by frequent ups and downs in valuations and/or outright crises (see Chapters 5 and 6).

iv Weakening of the influence of the national state and organizations of civil society on the cultural sector and particularly the art market. This is reflected in the reduction of public sector budgets for the arts.

v Increasing use of special tax jurisdictions (e.g. tax havens and freeports) to store works of art by private investors.

Equipped with increased income and wealth, the super-rich dominate the art market pushing up prices and leading to its growing segmentation. Profits of top galleries and large auction houses increase along with the revenues of top artists that are lucky enough to sell their works in the high segment.

Overall economic globalization has also led to art market globalization. The proliferation of art galleries with branches in different countries and international art fairs such as Art Basel, Venice Biennale and others helped in this process.

A feature of economic globalization has been the increasing frequency of financial crises and overall economic turbulence. Examples of these trends are the Latin American debt crises of the 1980s, the Asian crisis of 1996–1998, the Mexican crisis of 1994, the Argentinean crisis of 2001–2002, the global financial crisis of 2008–2009 and a score of national crises. The COVID-19 crisis has been also a global crisis with both health and economic dimensions. This has an impact on the art market as investors seek new ways of protecting their wealth from sharp fluctuations in asset prices. Artwork, like gold and precious metals, started to be seen as a potential "safe-haven" to counter-act financial volatility in other markets. Chapter 6 explores empirically this issue for the period 1998–2018.

In the 21st century, like in previous historical periods, changes in economic importance of superpowers also alter the core art markets, globally. The US art market has been the largest in the world for decades followed by the British, French and German markets. However, the American hegemony in the art sector started to be challenged by the rapid emergence of the Chinese art market, a phenomenon taking place since the early 2000s (see chapter 3).

The American dominance in the art world can be linked to several factors such as the large size of the US economy in which segments of the population hold substantial purchasing power and wealth that is channelled to the acquisition of artwork. Two other contributing factors are the American large infrastructure of galleries and auction houses and, very importantly, the existence of a favourable tax and regulatory frameworks regarding the arts that provide important benefits to develop an art market.

The story of the emergence of modern art markets in the East is interesting. Between 1949 and the 1970s, the East Asian art market was dominated mainly by Hong Kong. After the Chinese revolution triumphed most art dealers and art collectors in mainland China moved to Hong Kong, then a British overseas territory. The prevailing British legal code gave commercial security to galleries and auction houses; as a result, regional wealthy collectors turned to the island of Hong Kong to trade in the arts. Later, in the 1970s and 1980s, the East Asian art market was dominated by Japan. This country had experienced high rates of economic growth for decades, and managed to accumulate assets from the rest of the world (running balance of payments surpluses); its stock and real estate market boomed, and the yen was appreciated against main Western currencies, making it cheaper to buy Western art. These trends favoured the acquisition of impressionists and post-impressionists by Japanese collectors rising the importance of Japan in the global art collecting scene.

In the early 1990s, its art market, however, crumbled. Japan's stock market collapsed, and the economy entered a long period of stagnation with depressed asset prices (equities and real state) that destroyed large amounts of financial wealth, leading to plummeting sales by Japanese art galleries and auction houses.

Since the early 2000s, China has turned into the main Asian art market following super-rapid Chinese growth, a process accompanied by the formation of a middle-class, poverty reduction but also the concentration of wealth at the top of the distribution, in small economic elites of millionaires and billionaires. Main galleries and auction houses have been established in its main cities, and the number of auction houses has sharply increased. China's State Administration of Cultural Heritage issued new management measures for the Auction of Cultural Relics in late 2016, in which some regulations concerning

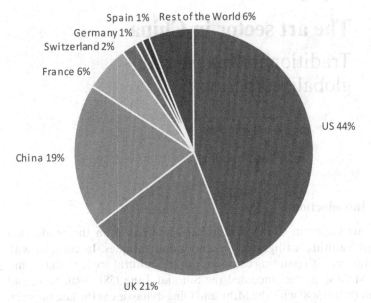

Spain 1%   Rest of the World 6%
Germany 1%
Switzerland 2%
France 6%
China 19%
US 44%
UK 21%

Figure 2.1 Global art market share by value in 2018.

Source: Own elaboration using data from art market 2019.

selling cultural relics were relaxed and procedures for applying for auction licenses in the art market were simplified. As a result of this, the country saw a sharp increase in the number of auction houses, with 13 new houses registering with the Chinese Auctioneers Association in only one year.[13]

The Hong Kong market has remained active along with the sprawl of galleries and the coming of western auction houses in mainland China.[14] Other important emerging regional art markets are Russia, India and Latin America.[15] As of 2018, the United States, United Kingdom and Chinese markets combined explain near 85 percent of global art market sales (Figure 2.1).

13 McAndrew (2018, p. 112).
14 McAndrew (2019), Hiraki et.al. (2009) and Bossier et al. (2014).
15 See Kraeussl and Logher (2010) and Edwards (2004) on the Latin American art market.

3 The art sector in China

Traditional, Maoist and globalized periods

3.1 Introduction

The art sector in China, historically, was based on the production of ink painting, calligraphy, ceramics and antiques. In contrast with Western art, oil painting came later to the cultural scene in that country. Main dynasties included the Sui and Tang (581–960), Song and Yuan (960–1368) with the Ming and Qing dynasties of the late imperial China (1368–1911). The late imperial era finished in 1911.

The modern China period covers from 1911 to 1949. Then in 1949, it came the triumph of the Chinese socialist revolution a process that followed a "long march" starting in the late 1920s with the government of the Kuomintang and the Sino-Japanese conflicts of the 1930s. Western art and Japanese art had a large influence over China during the period 1911–1949 intermingling with more traditional forms of art.

The ruling political leader and ideological figure from 1949 until his death in 1976 was Mao Tse Tung, a charismatic guide that exerted a strong influence on Chinese society. The Maoist period was characterized by adopting a brand of highly egalitarian communism, the priority given to mass education, access to health services and the mobilization of the population around progressive national goals. The country embarked on costly experiments such as the "leap-forward" of the late 1950s and early 1960s and the "cultural revolution" of the 1966–1976 period. The country invested in industrialization and the building of basic infrastructures such as electricity, roads, bridges, highways and the modernization of ports and other activities. Ideologically, individualism and class differences were not tolerated, and different methods were used to generate allegiance to official party line. In the 1950s, the Soviet Union was considered as the role model both in politics, the economy and cultural affairs but this started to change later in the decade and in the early 1960s.

DOI: 10.4324/9781003215127-3

Mao, however, was distrustful of Nikita Khrushchev's "revisionist" model that tolerated material privileges for the ruling elites and the use of material incentives to boost labour productivity that could lead to inequalities that were at odds with the egalitarian orientation of Chinese socialism.

In the late 1970s, after Mao's demise and the end of the tumultuous decade that followed the cultural revolution, the new political leadership changed course with important implications for the economy and cultural activities. At economic level, the idea of a modest living standard shared more or less equally by all was replaced by a tolerance of a degree of inequality to incentivize wealth creation. On the external side economic autarky and isolation were replaced by an opening towards foreign direct investment coming from advanced capitalist nations. In turn, Chinese products started to compete in international markets given their comparative advantages in light manufacturing based on low labour costs. A peculiar combination of communist party rule and increasing presence of foreign multinationals created a new form of market socialism with features of state capitalism very different from the China of the Mao era.

Three periods can be distinguished from the viewpoint of the art sector:

a   In the 1950s and early 1960s, the type of artwork encouraged was "socialist realism" largely defined by the Stalinist period in the USSR, adapted to the artistic realities and traditions of China.

b   The cultural revolution, from 1966 to 1976, in which politics and allegiance to Mao took primacy over economic considerations led to the mobilization of art as a tool of political mobilization and ideological purity was intensified.

c   In the globalized (post-Mao) China period, there was a return to more personal art motives moving away from political propaganda; Western art started to reassert itself again, but dissident art was not welcome by the party bureaucracy and government. In the 1990s, China started to be viewed as a potentially large and interesting market for art given the country's long artistic tradition and potential purchasing power in art as the economy was growing very rapidly, leading to the formation of an enlarged upper-middle-class and a tier of increasingly wealthy people that could buy artwork. International auction houses such as Sotheby's and Christie's held auctions in the early 1990s in mainland China along with Hong Kong and Taiwan. In the 2000s, the Chinese art market took off, reaching second/third place as share of total sales, alternating with the United Kingdom in terms of global sales of artwork (as said, the United States is the largest art market both in terms of sales and number of transactions worldwide).

3.2 Traditional Chinese art

The motives and tools of traditional Chinese art include calligraphy, ink and water-washing paintings, hanging scrolls and hand scrolls, ceramics, sculptures and other means. Main motives include landscapes birds, flowers, mountains (shan), rivers (shui), the figure of emperors, the teachings of Confucius, palace ladies, scenes of court life and horses. Confucian and non-Confucian philosophies and traditional religious beliefs such as Taoism and Buddhism influenced the content of artwork besides their impact on the political orientation of the various dynasties.

The Taoist love of nature, the Buddhist principle of emptiness along with the Confucian tradition of human cultivation and learning have in different ways shaped the type of painting and other forms of art in China. The pervasive presence of mountains, rivers and forests gave rise to the concept of "art as cartography" in Chinese art an encompassing concept including "art in maps" and "maps in arts".

Calligraphy[1] – the art of beautiful writing – occupies an important place in Chinese culture both as a means of communication and as a form of art. Calligraphy is taught at an early age to children in China and calligraphic works are expected to convey a sense of balance, proportion, variety, harmony, continuity and rhythm. Calligraphy is strongly guided by considerations of aesthetic value and is carried out through brushstrokes rather than pens. The grace in the use of the brush can be critical to determine its quality.

Furthermore, calligraphy is often used in poetry and immortalized thoughts. It was produced, chiefly, by the "literati" – aristocrats and scholar-officials – who were a sophisticated segment of the social structure endowed with leisure time to devote efforts to the cultivation of art and the conveying of feelings and ideas through literary texts and poetry. Calligraphy enabled a marriage between the visual arts and language, a symbiosis that is not often found in Western art.

Calligraphic expressions have changed through history. The characters are used not only in books, paintings, scrolls and posters but

1 Tingyou (2003).

also accompany architectural works, temples, public buildings and so on. It is present in public places such as parks, roads and avenues.

Paper, silk and textile fabrics are often used as supports for ink (black) paintings complemented by gouache and watercolours. The finished work can be mounted on scrolls and hung. Traditional painting can also be done on walls, porcelain and lacquerware.

Stylized landscapes want to convey "rhythm" and emotions stemming from nature rather than striving for very realistic depictions of physical landscapes. For this purpose, monochromatic and sparse colour is used.

A painting may be accompanied by a red zeal, used to identify artists and collectors and calligraphic characters. In the Chinese artistic tradition, there is not a strict separation between texts and painting; both forms of expressing ideas, concepts and feelings can come together. In addition, watercolours and gouaches are more widely used than oil painting. Paintings were oriented, historically, mostly to satisfy the aesthetic demands of the royal court, emperors, the higher public bureaucracy of the state and rich patrons. In that sense, during the various imperial periods, art was connected mainly to the wishes and patronage of the elites rather than the demand of the majority of the population.

Under the Ming dynasty (1368–1644) there were various art schools such as the Yuan School, the Wu school and the Zhe school. At the time of the Qing school (1644–1911), a market for art in a modern sense was not very important and often the *monetization of artwork* was *not* regarded as compatible with the high spirit and sophistication of art.

Still, the growing importance of commerce at the start of the industrial age could not be discarded. In the 18th and 19th centuries (Qing Dynasty), important commercial cities such as Yangzhou and Shanghai became also artistic centres. In those urban centres painters could offer their art and benefit from the support of wealthy merchants and patrons. In the late 19th century and early 20th century up to World War I, it took place the so-called "first wave of globalization"[2] with increasing interdependence across countries through international trade, global finance and international migration to also connect national art markets. These new winds also blew up on China.

After the end of the Qing dynasty in 1911, a score of artists and intellectuals went to Japan, Europe and the United States to study

2 Solimano (2010).

art-making and art history. Upon their return to China, they brought western influences that shaped the local art sector. They helped to bring to China western currents such as Impressionism, post-Impressionism, Fauvism and Cubism.[3] For the following decades until the revolution of 1949, traditional Chinese art, Japanese art and western aesthetic influences all were critical in shaping the art scene of the period.

The cultural influence of Japan on China was important at least until the Sino-China wars of the 1930s. Japan was an attractive source of inspiration as it had managed to incorporate western artistic influences within a Japanese idiom. Ink and brush painting propagated during the 1911–1949 period of modern China. Calligraphy reflecting gracious brush strokes was again incorporated into the art scene in this period. The *trilogy of mind, hand and paper* was important in defining cultural practices.

In the Chinese cultural environment, there is a dual appreciation of both the *end-result* of a painting or other form of art and the *process* through which an artwork is produced. To this, the tradition of *literati* painting (intellectual painting) encouraged artists to present their views and rationalizations of their own art. A common social practice was for an artist to invite friends at home to have tea and comment on their art, exchanging views between the artist and his or her audience. As said, including a text within a painting is common and it is often referred to as "written painting".

Nonetheless, showing and discussing art in private homes was not enough to spread art to a broader public. In 1929, the nationalist government in Nanjing (then the capital of China) organized the first art public exhibit in the city. In the 1930s, the Storm Society and the Art Wind Society organized exhibits of western-inspired art made by Chinese artists in Shanghai, a very cosmopolitan place with strong colonial ties and presence of British, French, American and Japanese colonies.[4] In the 1940s, the Shanghai Municipal Art Gallery played an important role to institutionalize art exhibits although the political uncertainties of that decade made it more difficult to fully complete these plans.

---

3 The case of Qi Baishi who started as a modest peasant and then became a great master instructed in the new trends of Western art intermingled with more traditional Chinese art is a case at hand.
4 Joy and Sherry (2004).

3.3 Art and revolution: Maoist China, 1949–1976

The triumph of the revolution of 1949, with a social base in the peasantry, brought significant departures from the prevailing art arrangements and conceptual orientations. Existing private galleries were, for the most part, subsumed in cultural institutions put in place by the new regime. It was given priority to state-owned galleries presenting art that fitted well into the new socialist ideology. From 1949 to 1976 traditional art style in its different varieties was replaced by the re-education of artists in the notion that art was a tool of political mobilization geared to the building of a highly egalitarian socialist society, with the hegemony of the Chinese Communist Party under the leadership of Mao. The Chinese Artists' Association (CAA), fully reorganized in 1953, played an important role in this process along with the Central Academy of Fine Arts of Beijing that set the model for other fine art academies in the country.

Mao's early views on art can be found in 1942 "Talks at Yunnan Forum on Literature and Art". In that lecture, Mao stated that art was directly related and shaped by the social and political conditions under which it develops: art and politics could not be dissociated. After the triumph of the revolution, socialist realism prevailed with its depictions of production achievements, mass rallies, heroic behaviour of the youth, cult to the maximum leader and so on.

The decade of the 1950s witnessed important changes in Chinese society, including a considerable degree of policy experimentation. International events in the socialist block such as Khrushchev's denunciation of the Stalinist period and the Hungarian uprising of 1956 prompted China's demands for relaxing the communist party's grip on society. It was demanded more personal autonomy in particular of intellectuals, artists and people in the cultural sector.

Social unrest also reached the working classes. According to an empirical study (Perry, 1994) in 1957, there were over five hundred labour disturbances and strikes in factories in Shanghai, a number above the historical records of labour strikes that occurred in the same city before the revolution, particularly in the 1920s and 1930s.[5] As a response to the demands for more political relaxation, Mao's launched the "One-hundred Flowers Campaign" encouraging open criticism of party practices, state action and bureaucratic mentality. As criticism mounted, there was a backlash and the degrees of freedom in

---

5 Perry (1994).

the art sector were reduced. In addition, the economy and society suffered famines and other dislocations, after the failure in the "Great Leap Forward", a strategy of development of popular communes and labour-intensive industrialization oriented to increase agricultural production to feed people in the country-side and cities. In this period, theatre and popular operas, generally highly accomplished in their display, also became an important tool of political propaganda through the arts. In 1965, it was created the China National Gallery of Art of 16,000 square meters in Beijing. It was a large gallery oriented to hold big artistic exhibitions.

Then in 1966, it came the cultural revolution that mobilized the youth. The "red guards" unleashed criticism and, at times, harassment of intellectuals, party officials and state cadres under the accusation of entertaining conservative views and right-wing tendencies. There was a search for purely "proletarian values" and the consolidation of uniformity in political outlooks under the guidance of Mao Zedong's ideas.

The cultural revolution targeted "four old": old customs, old culture, old habits and old ideas. This triggered actions, often by the red guards, that could do damage to ancient buildings, antiques, old books and artefacts. The room for tolerance and openness in the arts during the cultural revolution was very limited.

3.4 The post-Mao period

After Mao passed away and winds of renewal appeared over Chine society, new artistic trends started to develop. We can distinguish at least three painting groups that became associations or societies that departed from the official social realism of the Maoist period:

a   The Wuming (no name) painting association.
b   The XingXing (star-star) painting society.
c   The Caco-She (grass) art society.

The *Wuming* (no name) Painting Group established in Beijing was formed by artists of urban working-class background – most of them working in industrial factories that after work hours, weekends and holidays devoted their free time to painting. They entertained a sort of "apolitical art" in the sense of distancing themselves from the official ideology that "art serves politics" promoted since Mao's revolution.

The group held unofficial exhibits in homes or (discreet) public places in 1974, 1978 and 1981.[6]

Their paintings depicted personal motives and underscored emotional effects of political turmoil following the leap forward and the cultural revolution campaigns led by the state. Paintings of this group typically showed themes such as homes (Li Shan), flowers, simple landscapes, portraits, water and moonlight as more intimate reflections. The art served as personal refuge from the effects of societal change, directed from the political power that was intrusive of the private lives of the Chinese.

The XingXing (stars group) was created in 1979. It was initially formed by five artists and later the group expanded to 30 people. They constituted part of a Chinese avant-garde and their work included oil painting, ink painting, carved wood artefacts, watercolours and sculptures. In their activities, they linked also to literary groups, poets and philosophers. In their first exhibition in 1979 they presented Mao's carved face, *Idol* by the sculptor Wang Keping in which Mao resembles an old China emperor. This was shocking for a country that had embraced the deification of Mao just a few years ago. The exhibit took place in a small garden of the China National Gallery but on the third day, the show was declared illegal and had to be removed. In the 1980s, however, the XingXing Painting Society became officially registered and could present shows in the China National Gallery.[7] Nonetheless, their place in the art scene was vulnerable and eventually, some members of the XingXing group were barred to exhibit their art because of their un-conforming political views.

The Cao-Cao She (Green society) was established in Shanghai before their first exhibit in 1979. Shanghai, historically a sophisticated and cultured city that still had a pool of pre-cultural revolution artists, provided a more congenial place for the development of the arts than the more bureaucratic Beijing. The Cao-Cao She group maintained an active interest in new ink paintings; in part, they were inspired by European modernism and other trends different from socialist realism in the arts. The group promoted autonomy and individualistic aesthetics. Paintings, oil and ink, included landscapes, still life inspired in Impressionism and post-Impressionism along with abstract art with roots in Cubism and even abstract expressionism.

6 Want (2014/4).
7 Goodman (2011).

An important member of the group was Qiu Deshu, an art theoretician and painter, who developed abstract painting. However, his independent stance in politics and art brought him hostility from the authorities. The Green Society eventually dissolved itself in the early 1980s as a consequence of the lack of state support for their artistic activities and the problems faced by Qiu Deshu from official cultural circles.

The new cultural and political developments taking place in post-Mao's China attracted some international celebrities. Andy Warhol, an international representative of *political pop,* visited China (Hong Kong first then Beijing) in October of 1982. This was the one and only visit to the country by the artist.[8]

Warhol had already developed artistic work related to China. In 1972, the year President Richard Nixon went to China, Warhol started to paint his series of Mao portraits – completing near 200 pieces in ten years – based on his iconic image.

These portraits became a real hit in the west. A critical observer of fashions and, in general, of the marketing industry, Warhol noted, and apparently liked the simplicity of the blue clothing that was bear by almost everybody in China at that time, an egalitarian trait opposed to west's consumer society.

Political Pop was one of the artistic trends that started to emerge in post-cultural revolution China. A list of new art groups is the following:[9]

- Scar art
- Red brigade
- Nativist realism
- Cynical realism
- Rational printing
- Stream of life
- Political pop
- New generation
- Abstract expressionism

The aesthetic origins of these groups are varied. Several of them reflected the search for more individual motives, social criticism of

8 In a way Warhol's simple aesthetic and replication of ever-present imagery contributed to fusing pop and cultural revolution-era propaganda into what is known as "political pop".

9 Source: Modern art in China, facts and details. www.factsanddetails.com

the Maoist period, official ideology and Chinese iconography. Overall, they shared the quest for free creativity and the need to express the hardships inflicted on artists and intellectuals during the years of the cultural revolution. Particularly, that was the case of the Scar Art and Cynical Realism groups, among others. The diversity of perspectives and approaches to art and society of these different clusters is evident and this started to reshape the art landscape in China, giving the sector a new freshness and vitality.

3.5 De-politicizing of society in the 1990s and the boom in the art market of the 2000s

The 1990s was a decade in which China made important strides in integrating into the global economy both in trade and international investment. Now capitalist motivations, so scorned in the Maoist period, such as earning handsome profits became an engine for material prosperity in a country that until recently had staked on a completely different social and economic model. Multinationals from western countries started to arrive in large numbers driven by the expectation of producing manufacturing goods at a low cost that could be sold in global markets very competitively by taking advantage of an abundant labour force that had a reasonably good educational level; further, these labour contingents were disciplined by the state with a low probability of emergence of labour conflict. At the same time, this was a period of market development with the population adjusting to the emergence of new values that accepted competition, social differentiation and money-making. However, these developments were to take place in a still predominant socialist society operating under a planned framework.

Inequality of incomes and living standards rose and people started to face a degree of individual choice in consumption. This represented, no doubt, a sharp departure from the egalitarian logic of the 1950s, 1960s and 1970s.

A market for artwork begun to develop in Beijing, Shanghai, more so in Hong Kong with an increasing density of galleries, auction houses and the participation of art critics, curators and art scholars that could pass judgements on the quality of the artwork and advice new buyers domestic and foreign. A new artistic ecosystem developed.

In the early 1990s, the Chinese art market became also more global. International auction houses such as Christie's, Sotheby's and Phillips de Pury organized art shows in Beijing and Hong Kong. Domestic auction companies such as China Guardian and the Poly Group, linked in their origin to the Popular Liberation Army became important participants in the Chinese art scene. Overseas, the Poly Auction house opened offices in Manhattan, San Francisco, Sydney and Tokyo. In turn, China Guardian opened venues in the United States, Canada and Japan. These state-owned corporations were instrumental in enabling the export of Chinese art around the world.

The tracking of prices for artwork developed and Artprice reports on the Chinese market started to be published regularly since the 2000s. This knowledge of prices helps the market mechanism as objects traded are heterogeneous and information asymmetries can be serious. Since the mid-2000s, Christie's and Sotheby's established operations in China under a licensing system that encouraged the formation of joint-ventures with locally based auction houses although in the mid-2010s Christie's run its own independent venture.

At the same time, there began to emerge an increased domestic demand from Chinese collectors and buyers for western masterpieces including Monet, Picasso, Modigliani, Chagall, Damian Hirst and others. These sales were often intermediated by international auction houses.

A Chinese demand for Western art was virtually inexistent up to the 1980s and even the 1990s. The new collectors were, mostly, in the age groups of 30–50 years old. They belonged to a segment of socially mobile and economically prosperous people that was benefitting from a more globalized, market-oriented China.

Auctions typically cover three main segments: paintings and calligraphy, ceramics and antiques and contemporary art. Prices of contemporary art started to increase more strongly than the other categories. A rise in art prices took place in the period 2004–2008 with a large correction in 2009 at the time of the international financial crises. Nonetheless, certain regulations affect the Chinese art market. For example, they generally restrict the selling of artwork produced before 1949 precluding international auction companies to trade in objects considered as cultural heritage (Cultural Heritage Resource, 2009).

Summing up, we can attribute the increasing demand for Chinese art since the 2000s to at least five factors: (i) a surge in interest in the west in Chinese art by collectors and other participants of the art sector coinciding with the rising exposure and integration of China to global markets; (ii) a boost in international mobility of people going to China for tourism and business visits that in the field get exposed to Chinese art, (iii) the spread of interest on Chinese modern art by expatriates with purchasing power living in Hong Kong, Taiwan and Singapore; this group became active art collectors, (iv) the creation of a new segment of western-educated Chinese who returned to their home-country after attending universities in the United States, Europe, Australia to obtain master's degrees and PhD's and who have developed a new appreciation for art both produced in China as well as in the west. These people now manage in foreign languages and get more exposure to western culture; (v) the increasing prosperity of a segment of upper-middle class and rich individuals within China following the increasing marketization of society and the rapid economic growth experienced by the Chinese economy in recent decades. This new economic elite has developed an active demand for luxury goods (cars, jewellery, luxury apartments) and artwork. Nowadays, there is a score of Chinese citizens in the billionaires list of Forbes group who invest in art.

In terms of motivations for holding art in China, the evidence provided by research based on interviews of art dealers and companies operating in the art sector in China and Hong Kong[10] shows a combination of aesthetic motives and a new appreciation of art as an investment asset that can protect portfolio values in face of financial volatility and macroeconomic cycles.

---

10 (Zenya) National Wan, Kwan (2017) "China's Demand in works of Art and Six typologies of Chinese collectors in Four Groups", Haute Ecole de Gestion de Geneva.

4 Main features of the art market
What is art? How to value it?
How art trade is organized?

4.1 Introduction

Although our focus is mainly on the art market a distinction has to be made between the "art sector" and the "art market". The former is a broader concept than the latter. The art sector involves the role of the public sector in art through public museums, cultural policy, regulations and direct support to artists. In addition, there is a segment constituted by the not-for-profit sector that comprises art cooperatives and not-for-profit galleries and independent museums.

We can define the "art sector" comprising at least three segments or circuits:

a   The first circuit is a private market dominated by the forces of supply and demand for artworks with its own peculiarities as discussed below.
b   A second circuit includes a public segment dominated by public museums, public galleries and public institutions managing cultural policy.
c   A third circuit is formed by not-for-profit art organizations such as artistic cooperatives, small galleries and artists organizations.

Actors such as curators, art critics and scholars interact within and among these three segments through their critical assessment of artwork. They also provide analysis and opinions through specialized magazines and the press and give advice to museums and galleries, providing "legitimation mechanisms" to the art sector. In turn, laws and regulations (taxes, provenance rules and so on) also affect the cultural sector although this is considered not a very regulated sector.

DOI: 10.4324/9781003215127-4

4.2 Anatomy of the art market

Let us look at, briefly, the anatomy of the art market shaped by the forces of supply and demand although, as noted in previous chapters, this is a market with a significant degree of segmentation and transaction costs. The total demand for art is the sum of the demand from the private sector (profit and non-profit) plus the demand from the public sector. In turn this is decomposed in various sub-sectors:

a   Households (private collectors and other buyers).
b   Private museums and firms.
c   The public sector: from public museums that acquire paintings, sculptures, objects for their own collections (public and private).
d   The not-for-profit sector.

In some historical period, governments have been active in buying art; for example, during the New Deal of the 1930s in the United States, publicly the federal and state government acquired artwork that was devoted to post offices and decorate public buildings. In Mexico, the government in the 1920s commissioned murals to embellish public buildings and as a tool for maintaining the socially transformative mystique in the population that generated the revolution of 1910.

The supply of artwork comes from:

a   The *flow* of art production, say new paintings, new prints, new sculptures and so on from living artists.
b   The existing *stock* of artwork by dead and alive artists traded in the secondary market.

The actual working of the market is influenced by other actors, practices and institutions. Art experts, scholars and art critics all shape views on artists and thus influence the price of their work in the market through their opinions, essays and publications in books and the media. They also provide direct advice to collectors, museums and galleries. These influences can affect the demand and supply for art and therefore price formation. This "knowledge tier" or "intelligentsia" of the art market also influences the policies adopted by ministries of culture, public museums and other government agencies.

As shown in Chapter 2, historically, dealers and auction houses have been important players in the art market playing critical roles in the *intermediation* between supply and demand for art. In the modern age of the internet, technology also plays a role through online exhibits, online sales and the verification of authenticity of artwork through blockchains.

The online reconversion of the art market has been accelerated by the COVID-19 pandemic that has placed serious restrictions on the physical presence of people in galleries and auction houses. In addition, the rapid expansion of the financial markets and the proliferation of new financial instruments since the 1970s (financial globalization) are affecting the art market in new ways. Until recently, obtaining a loan from a bank to buy a painting was a rarity. Now, increasingly, a person can borrow to buy an expensive painting, using the acquired painting as a collateral to get the loan from the bank (other collateral may be required). Nowadays, commercial and investment banks are building their own in-house knowledge and marketing capacities related to art.

At the same time, other vehicles have appeared such as hedge funds and art funds specialized in investing only in art. This artwork may have different origins: American, European, Chinese and other countries and regions. These specialized funds typically earn a *management fee* (typically between 1 and 3 percent of the assets) and take a percentage of the fund's profits (say, 20–25 percent).[1] Fund's in turn have to cover the commissions charged by art dealers and auctioneers and pay taxes. Art funds build and manage important collections with the purpose of increasing the financial value of these collections.

Financial experts that traditionally provided advice on how to form a portfolio composed mostly of financial assets, now provide also advice to wealthy collectors on which type of art to acquire in order to maximize the expected profitability (adjusted by risk) of a portfolio. In addition, a financial expert will point out that art can be expected to diversify a portfolio to the extent that the prices/returns of financial assets and the return on holding art are not highly correlated in the same direction (diversification, to work, needs negative or zero correlation between the returns of the assets that compose a portfolio). The financial techniques of *art collateralization* (investment backed by an art object) and *art securitization* (selling divisible claims of an artwork) are increasingly used in the trading of art in the more sophisticated art markets.[2]

---

1 Investors put money into the fund and wait until collecting the returns from the fund's selling of the investment made in various types of art.
2 Deloitte (2017).

4.3 Art according to art critics and art historians

A perennial question is what is art? The Russian writer Leon Tolstoy in his book *What is Art* defined it as the mean of communicating emotions and subjective feelings. The famous British art historian, painter, critic and administrator Roger Fry (1926 [1999])[3] – attached to the Bloomsbury group in London at the time of Virginia Wolf, John Maynard Keynes and other intellectuals – said that defining art is rather complex and valid definitions range from Tolstoy's concept of art to a much simpler definition such as "(art is) is imitating solid objects upon a flat surface by means of pigments".[4] On the other hand, in ancient Greece, Plato, decided that paintings may not be that worthwhile after all and that artists could be dispensed of from his ideal republic.

Turning to a depiction of the art market Roger Fry offered his own classification of the demand for art as composed of three types:

a   The demand from "ignorant individuals" (or the philistine) who act unpredictably.
b   The men of culture who act with extreme caution. To this group, we may add scholars and art critics.
c   The snobs who act following the fashions of the day.

In a way, Fry's Philistine are equivalent to the unsophisticated investor in the stock market. In contrast, the "men of culture" would be the rough equivalent of financial experts and scholars. On the other hand, the snobs are people led by fashions rather than aesthetic considerations and an informed assessment of an artwork based on the close study of art history and the work of the specific artist. Fry's snob resembles Keynes' investor who bets on securities based on "average opinions".

Regarding the role of public policy (at the level of local and national governments) in the art sector, Fry identified three main goals and activities that could guide this intervention:

a   Art education.
b   Direct employment of artists in public works.
c   The acquisition and preservation of art treasures.

---

3 Goodwin (1999).
4 Fry (1909 [1920]).

Art critic Clive Bell and art historian, museum director and broadcaster – Kenneth Clark, identified as the lasting contribution of a nation to human civilization their contribution to literature, paintings, music, sculptures, historic buildings and so on. Warfare, plagues, generals and politicians are easily forgotten but not valuable artwork. Art provides an antidote to the dehumanizing effects of events and features of capitalism such as the industrial revolution, the process of factory alienation and the presence of hyper-capitalist profit-seeking. In this line, measuring the economic development of a country only through current consumption and/or gross domestic product, the utilitarian criteria so cherished by welfare economics are only weak yardsticks of human achievement. Cultural heritage and artistic treasures carry more permanence as indicators of achievements of people, nations and civilizations according to these authors.

A second justification for the public support of the arts as rationalized by both Fry and Keynes is the notion that art is one of the few refugees – a (spiritual) safe haven – in modern societies busy accomplishing tasks of dubious validity such as conspicuous consumption, the accumulation of material goods, the race to build financial wealth, the private appropriation of land and valuable natural resources and so on. Art, in contrast, is linked to creative processes, imagination and innovation. These traits promote lasting human values and an appreciation of beauty.

Complex questions related to art have no simple answers: What is good taste? Should every picture tell a story? Can art be democratic? Clark reflected on these conundrums and concluded that an appreciation of art requires intellectual effort, but this should not be an obstacle for art to be available to everyone to appreciate. In other words, art (enjoyment) must be inclusive and democratic although, at the same time, intellectually demanding. A true civilization (Clark himself directed a famous BBC series called "Civilization" that was broadcasted in the United Kingdom in 1969) is identified by the way that it responds (or not) to these key questions.

4.4 Genius and creativity: View of economists

The patterns of genius and creativity in art production is a topic that has been discussed in the literature, particularly by economists.[5] Sometimes

5 See Ekelund et al. (2017).

creativity in mathematics, physics and sciences is contrasted with creativity in the arts, literature and poetry. The role of education both at home and in schools is an important factor in cultivating creativity but simple relations are hard to infer for the case of art. Troubled personalities may trigger artistic creativity later in life in certain artists (Van Gogh, Pollock).

The relation between the "productivity" of the artist (how many paintings an artist produces in a period of time and/or his/her ability to deliver "master-pieces") and age, or more precisely, the phase in artist's career life-cycle has been examined by David Galenson, a professor of economics at the University of Chicago.[6] Galenson specialized in the study of types and patterns of artistic creativity in the 20th century, stressing what he calls "conceptual revolutions", the role of market structures and innovation in the art sector.

In his research, Galenson has found that some artists produce their best works at an early stage in their careers while others reach their "peaks" later in life. He developed an influential typology between "experimentalist innovators" and "conceptual innovators". The experimentalists would record their findings and would proceed by trial and error while the conceptualists would use art to express emotions and ideas. The latter group would have produced their main achievements earlier in life than the experimentalists according to Galenson. The author classifies Cezanne, Rodin, Gorky, de Kooning, Pollock, Newman and Rothko as experimentalists while Picasso, Matisse, Liechtenstein, Rauschenberger, Stella and Johns as conceptualist innovators. Predictably, disentangling with great precision, which typology of creativity belongs to each artist is not a simple endeavour.

Economists also emphasize the role of monetary incentives in art production and highlight the deterring effects (at least in the short run) associated with the existence of barriers to entry in the art market. For example, the French impressionists could not present their artworks in the official salons in Paris in the 19th century and this, for a while, postponed their reach and eventual success in society. However, as innovations in the places of exhibiting their work were developed Impressionism became a dominant form of art, confirming that "innovation in market structures" can boost new forms of art.

6 Galenson (2009).

A more contemporaneous example could be the development of digital art and the role of top auction houses in this process.[7]

The (artistic) *homo-economicus*, say a cold calculator of costs and benefits, who allocates time and effort to the production of art in response to monetary incentives is far from the only model in the history of art. The "renaissance ideal" saw the artist as performing activities such as creation of beauty that were more elevated than pure pecuniary gain. In 1510, Leonardo da Vinci stated that "the glory of excellence of the mortals is much greater than of their riches". Earlier on, in 1435, Leon Battista Alberti had said that "A mind intent on gain will rarely obtain the reward of fame and posterity".[8] The fine producer artist, like the aristocrat (who buys art), worked for higher goals than money.

Political scientists and sociologists emphasize the role played by the social context in giving rise to new art schools and art tendencies. For example, abstract expressionism developed, mainly in the United States, during and after the destruction and horrors of World War II. Then, the rise of the consumer society, in the 1950s and 1960s, provided impetus for the development of pop art (Warhol, Lichtenstein). Warhol, originally engaged in the early 1960s in painting dollar bills, Campbell's cans, Marilyn Monroe's faces that alluded to mass consumption and the commercialization of celebrities' symbols. Nonetheless, it is worth noting that Warhol in spite of his reservations of consumer-driven capitalism had a favourable attitude towards money and wealth, commerce and business in his life, in a clear contrast with the Renaissance ideal that was highly influential in the art world for centuries. A similar view to Warhol is often attributed to Jeff Koons and Damien Hirst, post-Warhol innovator artists who strived for selling their artwork at the highest price possible. All of them considered the market as "the highest critic" of an artist's work.

7 In turn, it is a common staple that starting young artists (some of them with great potential) face problems to find galleries willing to display their work. In turn, artists who are not in favour of curators and critics also may face a hard time to sell their work to museums.
8 See Galenson (2007).

4.5 Special features of the art market

The rest of the chapter will be devoted to seven special features that make the art market different from other markets.[9]

4.5.1 Heterogeneity and indivisibility

Paintings, sculptures and drawings are unique and heterogeneous objects; they are not a substitute one for another: a painting by Claude Monet in the impressionist tradition cannot be easily compared with a Jackson Pollock work of abstract expressionism. They have different techniques, motivations were painted in different historical periods and cultural contexts.

In general, a work of art such as a painting and sculpture is not (physically) *divisible*. You cannot hang in your wall one-third of a Modigliani painting or half of the Da Vinci's Mona Lisa. However, art can be *financially divisible*: new financial techniques of *securitization* and *tokenization* (the issuing of digital tokens in a blockchain representing claims on an asset) seek to circumvent the physical division impossibility. A person may acquire, for investments purposes, only a share (say a 2 percent or less) of the value of an Andy Warhol work or of any other artist, in a similar fashion that an investor can own a fraction of an enterprise through buying a certain stocks of that company (claims on the net worth of the firm). Financially, a piece of artwork can be divisible in terms of claims on it and the pieces (claims) can be traded in a market; however, for purposes of aesthetic enjoyment, an art object is hardly divisible.

Indivisibility and heterogeneity issues have implications for constructing art price indices. Two main statistical methods have been devised: first, the *repeated sales regression method* (RSR) in which the purchase (sale) price of the *same art object* at least two times are compared. The repeated sales method is used to compute price variations and rates of return (the *real* rate of return is the percentage increase in the price minus overall inflation). The second method is the *Hedonic Regression* (HR) econometric methodology in which differences in quality and other characteristics of an art object such as height and width, painting technique, style, date and school of art,

---

9 Some of these features are discussed in economically oriented journal articles of the art market. This literature includes Baumol (1986), Korteweg et al. (2016), Mei and Moses (2002). Books on the art market of broader dissemination comprise Adam (2014, 2017) and Robertson and Chong (2018).

whether the artist is dead or alive and so on are taken into account in running econometric regressions of price determination as the dependent variable. The advantage of the HR method is that it avoids problems of small sample often present in the RSR method; however, a drawback of the HR method is its sensitivity to the specification of the regression that can lead to misspecification biases.[10] In addition, the most frequent source of art prices are auctions that also embed a bias since actual purchase or acquisition prices are not published, only sales prices. A reference price for comparisons of returns is the reservation price.

Newer methods for assessing and predicting prices of artwork are based on big data and artificial intelligence techniques, particularly the machine learning method that use large amounts of information (including descriptive dimensions of each artwork) to detect patterns and human emotions that shape the demand for art, at the time of valuing artwork (see Aubry et al., 2019).

An art collection that provides a unique database to understand the behaviour of art prices over time is that of John Maynard Keynes, the British economist who not only revolutionized the field of macroeconomics but also had an innate love for the arts and helped to found the Art Council in the United Kingdom in the early 1940s. As said, Keynes belonged to the Bloomsbury Group, formed by free-minded artists, writers, and intellectuals in the first three decades of the 20th century. Keynes's art collection has the advantage that preserved the same art objects (mostly impressionist and post-impressionist paintings) over time allowing to track the variation of prices of the *same* paintings without having to resort to special statistical techniques to control for changes in quantities and quality. It also helped the fact that Keynes was a very methodical person who kept detailed records of the most important features of each painting he acquired over his adult life, including, of course, their prices of acquisition and current prices. The collection is currently valued at around GBP (Great Britain Pounds) 70 million (he spent near GBP 13,000 in constant pounds in the acquisition of his art portfolio). The collection is currently located in Kings College and the Fitzwilliam Museum at Cambridge, England.

10 For more details see David (2014) and Renneboog and Spaenjers (2013).

4.5.2 The economic valuation of art and liquidity

The monetary valuation of art is not simple. An economist would say that value equals price. Nonetheless, as Oscar Wilde noted, this procedure (value = price) may seem close to his definition of the cynic as "a person who knows the price of everything but the value of nothing". Neoclassic theory of price determination is based on the interplay between demand and supply. The market demand for art is associated with the subjective appreciation and willingness to pay for a certain art object. Art demand reflects emotions that the view or use of a certain object triggers in people.

Some authors speak of the demand for art as *"aesthetic consumption"* (Mandel, 2009). Others stress that art is *symbolic consumption*, say the holder of art is interested in buying art to give a signal of wealth or cultural sophistication. In a way, art can be a "Veblen good", say a luxury good whose demand is upward sloping with respect to price. This is so since a higher price conveys a signal of socio-economic status that is positively valued by the buyer (of course at a pecuniary cost).[11]

The principle of "effective demand" that Keynes brought to macroeconomic analysis also applies to art. The budget constraint in a monetary economy implies that a person needs money to buy art (and other commodities). If prospective buyers do not have money/resources available (including borrowing possibilities) there will not be an effective demand for art. Therefore, the demand for art is bound to be a function of the income and wealth *levels* of the art buyers. Moreover, in the aggregate (the whole economy) the demand for art will also depend on the *distribution* of wealth and income among citizens. In addition, the demand for art will depend on the expected, risk-adjusted and return of holding art.

Prices vary according to characteristics such as medium (oil, watercolour, acrylic) in the case of paintings; clay, marble, iron in the case of sculptures, the size of the artwork, the date of its production and other characteristics. In turn, the supply of artwork by dead artists is fixed and the supply of living artists may not be that elastic to price, at least in the short run. Thus, we may expect that *changes in demand* will largely drive prices in the art market rather than changes in supply (although this may occur if dealers in the secondary market bring a greater stock of artwork to the market or if artists, lured by the expectations of higher sales, start painting in larger amounts).

---

11 See Veblen (1899) *The Theory of the Leisure Class.*

Selling art is not like selling bread. Sales are infrequent, particularly for masterpieces and high-value work. Moreover, the ability of a collector or buyer to convert a painting or sculpture into money at a low cost can be limited, particularly at times of economic downturns.[12] Thus, the art market is *not* a very *liquid market*. Normally, the ability of a collector or a dealer to turn an artwork into money is limited in the short run. Famous macroeconomists such as John Maynard Keynes, John Hicks, Hyman Minsky and others have shown that a modern capitalist economy is better described as a *complex monetary economy* rather than a barter economy.[13] In a monetary economy, goods are exchanged for money and money is used to acquire other goods. In a complex, large scale, economy *barter* – the direct exchange of goods for goods – is difficult and carry non-trivial transaction costs as it needs a matching of needs (demand) and availabilities of goods (supply) that is not easy to find.[14]

Keynes identified three main motives for holding money: (i) for financing transactions (buying food, paying rent, transportation and so on), (ii) as a precaution to face contingencies and (iii) for speculative purposes. This latter motive often requires being liquid (e.g. holding money) to be able to buy art at a convenient price if a good bargain appears. Incidentally, that was the case during World War I in Paris when Maynard Keynes, a public servant at the British Treasury at the time, managed to buy valuable post-impressionist paintings both for the British treasury and for his own private collection. The purchases were conducted at very convenient prices in which both the British Treasury and Keynes benefitted from the deals.

The lack of liquidity rises transaction costs as going from money to art and from art to money implies *search and authentication costs*. For an investor being "long" in art often implies a cost in terms of liquidity. In contrast, a person holding stocks and bonds can liquidate them if needed at low cost (for given prices) since in a modern monetary

---

12 Until recently, in the United States and other countries, the law did not allow a person to be owner of a portion of an artwork. Nevertheless, this is starting to change. In some countries, included now the United States, art investment funds are starting to offer people to own a "piece" of an artwork in similar fashion that a person can own a fraction of an enterprise by buying equities.

13 Hicks (1989), Keynes (1936), Minsky (1975, 1982, 1986).

14 Theoretical economic models developed by Wilfredo Pareto, Leon Walras and others often postulated "barter economies" to understand exchange in an abstract market system.

economy these are standardized financial products trading in well-organized markets. The same can't be said for artwork. There are some interesting parallels between the way prices are determined in the stock market and in the art market. A way of pricing capital is using the market valuation of stocks that are claims on the capital stock of a company. However, this procedure has engendered controversies in the theory of capital. Keynes and Minsky, for example, pointed to the prevalence of *arbitrary beliefs* and volatility in stock markets that makes price signals to an extent unreliable to assess the long-run value of capital. In a symmetric way, we may define the value of art as simply the market pricing of artworks. Again, if art markets are thin and subject to price manipulation market prices may be also unreliable indicators of long-run values.

The price of stocks may differ from their "fundamental/long run value" of investment – Keynes's famous marginal efficiency of capital – because of the inherent difficulty of assessing *future* profits due to the existence of inescapable uncertainty. An investor necessarily will make arbitrary valuations when buying a factory or when acquiring stocks since the value of these assets depends on the *present value* of future profits that simply can't be known with certainty at the time of buying the capital asset. Similarly, establishing prices for artwork is not simple, particularly in the case of emerging artists whose future production of art is uncertain in terms of quality and quantity.

Roger Fry proposed a solution to these riddles: he defined the long-run value of an artwork by its *value at posterity*. An example of how the difference between the "value at posterity" and the "spot market value" may differ by significant margins is provided by the paintings of Vincent Van Gogh. The story goes that, while Van Gogh was alive, he apparently managed to sell only one of his paintings, dying in dire poverty (he was financially supported during most of his adult life by his brother Theo). In contrast, now, his paintings are sold at extremely high prices (in tens or hundreds of million dollars). If Van Gogh were alive today, at the beginning of the third decade of the 21st century, he would be a very wealthy person as the market valuations of his paintings rose spectacularly between his lifetime and today (a high "value at posterity").

A source of deviations from the value at posterity is Fry's "demand of snobs" and the "demand by the ignorant", driven by current fashions rather than true aesthetic value. In Keynes' Chapter 12 of the *General Theory of Employment, Interest and Money* he developed the concept of "mass of ignorant people" (the equivalent of the art market snob) who makes average valuations in the stock market.

Summing up, although, in principle, a capital good has a "fundamental value" (the present discounted value of future profits) and an artwork does not have an obvious fundamental value both are subject to fundamental uncertainty and correct pricing remains a complex issue with no easy solutions.

4.5.3 *Transaction costs, search and illegal activities in the art market*

Returning to the issue of liquidity in the art market, it is important to recognize that transaction costs and (lack of) liquidity are related concepts. Exchanging money for artwork (buying art) and exchanging art for money (selling art) involve non-trivial transaction costs. The concept of transaction costs was pioneered by the economist Ronald Coase who pointed out that in the real world, market participants must allocate real resources (time, search efforts, quality assessments) to make transactions possible. Reaching a market equilibrium in which demand is equal to supply and the price remains stationary unless disturbed by a shock is not costless.

The significance of transaction costs, however, varies depending on the type of market. Buying oranges in a local market is very likely to entail lower transaction costs than purchasing a French impressionist painting of the 19th century or a Russian avant-garde piece of the 1920s. Buying these paintings is bound to imply incurring in high-transaction costs since making sure the paintings are original pieces rather than fake copies is costly. In the language of the art market, there are *authentication costs*: the costs of tracking the *provenance* of an artwork, say responding with accuracy to questions such as: Who was the artist? When and where he or she produced it? The history of selling and buying of the artwork – chain of ownership – is important to make sure the work is original (not a fake) and is in reasonably good shape. Therefore, art markets are affected by asymmetric information – the so-called "lemons problem" – in which sellers often have superior information than buyers on the quality and provenance of the piece they are selling (like the market for used cars or the market for used housing).

Recent technology associated with the cryptocurrency technology of blockchain, however, can help to reduce authentication problems. In particular, *non-fungible tokens* (NTF) that are digital representations of ownership of objects, both digital and physical, can greatly help in the validation of artwork. As NFT are built into the blockchain developed by Ethereum, the ownership and precedence of the artwork can be traced and verified and the buyer gets assurances that the piece has not been subject to manipulations. Tokenization is growing fast in particular in terms of ownership of digital art. As said before, the largest sale to the time of this writing of NFT linked to a piece of digital art is Mark Winkelmann's digital collage *Everydays: the first 5,000 days* sold by Christie's in U$69 million.

In turn, a dealer who receives a painting as a commission for sale must find a buyer, not an easy task. In turn, auction houses to sell must spend money in advertisement, preparing catalogues and organize the various tasks involved in an auction.

Another important factor that leads to increases in transaction costs is the presence of *illegal activities* in the art market. Three main irregularities in the market are:

- *Theft*: Artwork can simply be stolen from its owner and sold in the market, although, of course, there is legislation oriented to prevent the theft of artwork. According to Anglo-Saxon law, the purchase of a stolen work – whether the buyer knows its provenance or not – leaves the purchaser liable for the return of the piece stolen to the original owner or their representatives.
- *Faking*: this practice refers to replicating an artwork that has already been produced. The imitation may be portrayed as a copy or as the "original".
- *Forgery*: producing a work similar to that of an artist. This practice is also called "pastiche".

Illegal activities in the art sector affect the credibility of dealers, galleries, auction houses and even museums that may be displaying, unintendedly, faked/forged work (this practice may reach a far higher percentage than often believed). As it can be expected, false artwork can seriously undermine the use of art as an investment vehicle.

According to Ekelund et al. (2017), art theft mobilizes around U$6–10 billion annually in the black (art) market with the average frequency of recovery not exceeding 5–10 percent of the stolen artwork. In addition, average (black) market price of stolen art is estimated to be about 10 percent of the value of the work if it were traded, legally, in open markets.

It is interesting to note that art theft is considered the *third-largest criminal activity* in the world after drug dealing and illegal arms trade.[15] An important reason behind the blossoming of illegal art trade lies in its use as "money" (in its function of store of value) by drug dealers and arms traders to launder revenues coming from other illegal activities (drugs and arms trade for example).

Historically, during occupied Europe in World War II, high officials from the Nazi regime were main looters of art in the countries in which they were stationed (see Chapter 5).[16] In more recent times, the single largest art robbery took place on March 18, 1990 (St Patrick's day) at the Isabella Stewart Gardner Museum in Boston, Massachusetts, in which 13 pieces of art including Rembrandts (two), Vermeer, a Manet, Degas's drawing and other valuable works robbed. Up to now, the stolen paintings have not been recovered.

It is considered that the fight against illegal art market transactions is a relatively *low priority* for national governments, international police and investigative bodies. Right or wrong it is considered an elite concern of less importance than preventing street robberies, home assaults and drug dealing. In general, the market for art theft is growing over time as well as the transactions related to faked art and forgeries (both paintings and prints).[17]

4.5.4 The financialization and globalization of art markets

The transactions in the modern art market increasingly require financial supports and borrowing possibilities have increased as financial institutions are offering loans to their qualifying clients to buy art. A new financial ecosystem tied to the art market includes art investment funds, hedge funds, family offices, commercial banks investing in art, mostly on behalf of their wealthy clients.[18] Historically, art was bought by patrons with their own funds. In spite of authenticity and uncertain provenance, this financial ecosystem seems to be thriving and evolving in sophistication.

A basic task of financial analysis is comparing the rates of return, adjusted by risk, across different assets to detect the absence or presence of unexploited arbitrage opportunities. Nonetheless, from an

---

16 Nicholas (1995).
17 A well-known case of forgery affected two well know galleries in New York City between 1994 and 2009: this was the case of the Knoedler Gallery (founded in 1846, closing activities in 2011) and the Julian Weissman Gallery. The scam involved a lady under the name of Glafira Rosales who hired a former street painter, Pei-Shen Qian, with professional training in producing works copying Rothko, Pollock and Motherwell, to fake high-value paintings that she sold to these sophisticated galleries (for more details, see Chapter 6 in Ekelund et al., 2017).
18 See Deloitte (2017).

analytical perspective the calculations (in empirical studies) of rates of return of investing in art are subject to various technical difficulties:

a   Prices often come from *indirect methods* such as hedonic prices, the repeated sales method and big data techniques.

b   The exclusion of *unsold items* in auctions (artwork that fails to meet the reservation price asked by the seller). This can produce a sample selection bias that can be in the direction of inflating price calculations.

c   Empirical studies may fail to consider the *premium* paid by the buyer to the auction house when a "hammer price" is achieved.

d   Non-pecuniary benefit sometimes referred to as the "*psychic return*" represented by the consumption utility of enjoying art is not computed in the calculation of monetary rates of return. This element must be added to the *gross financial return* while the premium, or commissions, have to be deducted to obtain a *net* rate of return.[19] Of course, monetizing the "psychic return" is not easy.

Empirical studies using historical data of prices (often based on auctions) and changes in valuation of entire collections, such as the Keynes collection and studies that rely on repeated sales or hedonic pricing methods tend to show that the *average* rate of return (capital gains over acquisition values) from trading in artworks *does not* differ, substantially and in a systematic way, from the return of holding stocks or bonds once adjusted by risk premiums, in the medium to long run.[20] These studies include Campbell (2008) and Mandel (2009) that examine the correlation between artwork's average return and their variances and those of other financial assets and Kraeussl, Lehnert and Martelin (2014) that explores the possibility of bubbles in art prices in the period 1970–2013. In general, the standard deviation of art investment tends to be considerable and this goes against investment in art for risk-averse wealth holders.[21]

We have mentioned that artworks can serve as a *refuge – a safe-haven asset* – at times of depression, economic crises and overall uncertainty. In financial theory, a *safe haven asset or investment* is defined as an asset that is either uncorrelated or has a negative correlation with other assets of an existing portfolio. This feature of zero or negative

19 Burton et al. (2017).
20 Chambers et al. (2017); Worthington and Higgs (2004).
21 See David (2014).

correlation contributes to *diversifing* a portfolio as returns move in opposite directions. Within this framework, Solimano (2017) investigates the extent to which *gold* behaved as a "safe haven asset" during three main international slumps: the great depression of the 1930s, the stagflation of the 1970s and the global financial crisis of 2008–2009. In those episodes, stocks and real estate suffered losses in their economic value inducing investors to look for alternative assets. In contrast, the price of gold *increased* in these three international crises suggesting that indeed this precious metal behaved as a safe haven asset. Now with the COVID-19 crises, the price of gold has also appreciated in a substantial way (along with Bitcoin and Ethereum, the two main cryptocurrencies).

Now, the question is whether *art* can be a safe haven investment behaving in a *counter-cyclical* way in downturns (like gold). This issue is explored in more detail in Chapter 6. Existing evidence shows that *average* prices (and volumes) in the art market declined in the Great Recession of 2008–2009 in line with the fall, in those years, in the real price of stocks and the price of property. In that sense, the art market as a whole may have failed to serve as a safe haven/counter-cyclical asset in that specific international recessive episode. However, more research is needed to fully answer this question, as it is likely that some specific works of art (Old Masters and top contemporaneous artists) preserved and even increased their value in the crisis of 2008–2009 and in the COVID crises of 2020–2021. Assessing the safe asset feature of artworks requires estimating the *correlation* between art prices and equity and property prices *during business cycles and crises periods.*[22]

4.5.5 Concentration and polarization

The global art market shows features of a *polarized market* in which the bulk of the number of transactions (volume) is concentrated at the *lower end* of the market, (the lower-end is defined as artwork sold below U$50,000 a piece according to UBS-Art Basel annual reports on the global art market) while the bulk of *sales value* (prices times quantities sold) is concentrated at the *higher-end* of the market (prices above U$1 million, see Table 4.1). The *middle-range* of the market is between these lower and upper bounds. Polarization in the top tier is reflected, among other ways, in the dominant presence of the most

---

22 Solimano (2020) provides a historical analysis of many episodes of recessions and crises around the world in the 20th century and early 21st century.

Table 4.1 Share of lots sold and total value at global fine art auctions in 2017 by price bracket

	Value (percent)	Volume (percent)
Lower-end (Below $50k)	8.6	89.8
Middle market ($50k–$1m)	27.9	9.4
High-end (Above $1m)	63.5	0.9
Total	100.0	100.0

Source: McAndrew (2018).

important auction house and large galleries in the main international art fairs (that have become an increasingly important way to sell art) that take place in cities like New York City, Miami, Basel and London. They clearly outcompete middle and small-size galleries.

In the very high-end of the market, prices can reach *extravagant levels* as we noted in the Introductory chapter. Leonardo da Vinci's "Salvatori Mundi" (Jesus Christ as saviour of the world) a painting dated to c.1500 was sold for U$450 million in an auction held by Christie's in New York City in 2017.[23] The buyer was Prince Badr bin Abdullah Bain that acted, allegedly, on behalf of Abu Dhabi's Department of Culture and Tourism to be exhibit in Abu Dhabi's Louvre museum. Some mystery has surrounded the actual location of this piece in the years after its acquisition. The really astonishing price paid for Da Vinci's piece shows the big availability of financial resources of certain museums in rich nations.

Another painting that reached very high prices is Claude Monet's series called Haystaks, say stacks of harvested wheat (*Les Meules at Giverny,* in French, means stacks at Giverny, Monet's home in the Normandy, where he lived and painted during the last 30 years of his life). The oil painting (60 cm × 100 cm) was one of a series of Haystacks painted in 1890–1891 by Monet. This artist liked to paint the same object – a landscape, a cathedral, a scene – several times in different seasons of the year conveying distinct lighting and atmospheric conditions. The *Meules* was sold for U$110.7 million in 2019 in an auction by Sotheby's, the first impressionist painting to surpass the U$100 million threshold at that time.

---

23 This painting is reported to have been copied at least 12 times and restored a number of times during its lifetime.

It is important to note that the modalities for meeting buyers and sellers of artworks have changed over time, with visits to galleries declining in recent years and more so during the COVID pandemics. The *auction segment* (secondary market) – a traditional tool of selling art that dates back to the 17th century in London, (see Chapter 2) – accounted for almost half of the total fine art sales in 2017 (U\$28.5 billion of U\$63.7 billion, McAndrew, 2018, 16). This segment is also dominated by very few actors: the houses Christie's, Sotheby's, Poly Auction, China Guardian and Phillips de Pury.[24]

In a market dominated by big players, with a growing presence of the financial sector, the influence of the individual artist is diminished. Despite having created the value of the artworks in the first place, artists exert limited control on the destiny of their creation, resembling, to an extent, the popular notion of the worker affected by alienation in the capitalist factory system.

The upper-end of the art market is characterized by highly personal relations and at times obscure practices regarding price and fees (the buyers and seller's premiums) charged by the house in auctions; revealing episodes confirming these assertions can be found in Adam (2017; 2014). Information regarding the price at which the pieces are expected to sell can be subject to manipulation and may fail to reach all prospective buyers. Many times, the prices are set unrealistically low to attract potential buyers although on other occasions, the prices are inflated, detracting buyers from building interest in particular pieces – which are likely to be sold to preferential bidders. Prices of certain artists promoted by galleries can be also inflated. Moreover, the art market is increasingly converging towards a "winners-take-all-market", in which the high prices, profits and commissions are captured by a small minority of intermediaries and "superstar" artists –either living or dead/heirs – dominating the upper-end of the market. The "economics of superstars" in arts, sports and entertainment (Rosen, 1981) develops the notion that very big differences in earnings accruing to the "superstar" can coexist with relatively small differences in talent among market participants, leading to the "winners-take-all syndrome".[25]

24 The fine art revenue generated by Christie's and Sotheby's represented over 75 percent of the fine art revenue of the five mentioned houses in 2017 (McAndrew, 2018, p. 106).

25 Solimano (2008, 2010) expanded Rosen's framework to examine the global markets for talent in different fields such as scientific achievement, new technology, entrepreneurship, cultural activities and the health sector.

Table 4.2 The art market, the stock market and property markets

	Type of market		
Feature	Artwork	Stocks	Property
Valuation	Complex	Intermediate	Intermediate
Liquidity	Low/Increasing	High	Moderate /Low
Divisibility	Low (non-financial)	High	Low
Polarization	High	Moderate	Moderate/High
Regulation	Low	High	Moderate
Transparency	Low	High	Low/moderate
Transaction costs	High	Low	Intermediate

Table 4.2 summarizes various complex features of art markets regarding indivisibilities, transaction costs, liquidity issues, lack of transparency and market polarization. These features are compared with their incidence in stock markets and real estate markets.

Table 4.2 underscores the inherent problems faced by individuals and companies in the valuation of artwork, particularly pieces produced by young emerging artists and masterpieces that get to extravagant levels. In addition, the market is affected by liquidity issues (pieces are hard to convert into money in the short run); however, this feature is partly being relaxed by the appearance of new vehicles of art finance such as securitization, art loans and non-fungible tokens associated with the blockchain.

A typical trait of art markets is the physical indivisibility of art in contrast with its recent financial divisibility. Polarization between the high-end segment of large galleries and the mass of middle and small size galleries is another issue, along with opacity in market practices and transaction costs.

Valuation complexities present in the art market are shared, to some extent, with valuation conundrums in financial markets: spot price quotations of art and capital can be a poor proxy of their long-run values a complexity that extends to property markets that also trade long-lived assets. In turn, liquidity is larger in stock markets than in art markets with property markets probably lying in between these two markets.[26]

---

26 Well-organized mortgage credit markets have increased liquidity in the real estate market.

5 Recessions, financial crises and war

Impact on the art sector

5.1 Introduction

The history of capitalism is full of financial and macroeconomic cycles of boom and bust, expansions and recessions. Price bubbles arising at times of euphoria and over-optimism (these bubbles are cumulative, albeit transitory, deviations of prices from their fundamental values) when collapse can trigger debt defaults by firms and governments, distressing the banking system, cutting credit and inducing a collapse of the real economy. In turn, wars are instances of social breakdown that have not been infrequent events throughout history.

Famous speculative sprees include the tulip bubble (satirically painted by Jan Brueghel) and a high demand for shares of the Dutch East India company in 1636–1637; the Mississippi company and the Banque General in France in 1720; the speculation in South Sea Company stock (1720) and the high trade of Latin American bonds in 1825 in England. Examples include booming railroad stocks in 1873 in the United States, the appreciation in value of land and gold mines in Australia in 1893; the real estate boom in Florida (USA) in the early 1920s, the rise in equity prices in the second half of the 1920s up to 1929, the appreciation of gold values in the 1930s and late 1970s; the rise in high-tech stock values in the late 1990s in the United States, the real estate boom in Japan, Spain and Ireland in the 1980s; highly appreciated stocks in Iceland and property values in the United States between 2003 and 2007; the very rapid price increase of Bitcoin in 2017 and 2020–2021 and other examples.[1]

1 See Kindleberger (1978[2000]), Lerer and Mc Garrigle (2018) and Solimano (2020).

DOI: 10.4324/9781003215127-5

5.2 Crashes and art markets

An empirical study that examines the impact of the stock market crash of October 1929 on the art market in France (the most important world art centre at the time) is Rezaee and Sequeira (2018). The authors use standardized price data for more than 3000 modern paintings from over 1000 artists in the period January 1929 to June 1930 (before, during and after the stock market crash). The results show that both stock prices and art prices moved together, and both declined the months before and during the October crash. However, art prices recovered forcefully between January and June of 1930 while stock prices continued depressed in that period. The authors interpret this behaviour as a flight to safety by investors who abandoned stocks and shifted to artwork during a period of turbulence in financial markets.

Hyperinflation, a main monetary-disequilibria, has potential impacts on the prices of artwork. Hyperinflation is defined as very dramatic increases in the price of goods and foreign exchange – up to 50 percent per month or daily increases of 2–3 percent that last up to nine consecutive months. Episodes of hyperinflation in the last 100 years include rampant inflation in Germany, Austria, Hungary, Poland and Soviet Russia in the first half of the 1920s, Greece in the early to mid-1940s and Hungary again late in that decade; Bolivia, Argentina, Nicaragua and Peru in the 1980s, Yugoslavia in the early 1990s, Zimbabwe in 2008 and Venezuela in 2017–2020.[2] Unfortunately, we have little information on art prices during these episodes of explosive inflation. Nonetheless, it is likely that artworks managed to keep their real value much better than money during these cases of acute monetary disorder.

Recessions say declines in GDP, industrial production, investment, employment and international trade can also affect art prices. In a recession, on average, household incomes and the value of wealth decline potentially affecting the demand for artwork. *A History of Big Recessions in the Long Twentieth* summarizes 750 episodes of recessions around the world in the period 1900–2017[3] and shows that 56 percent of the cases correspond to declines in GDP per capita below 3 percent (moderate recessions) and 86 percent to declines below 10 percent (severe recessions). These episodes include a host of national episodes of recession, the global recessions of the 1930s

2 See Solimano (2020).
3 Solimano (2020).

and 2008–2009, the stagflation of the 1970s, regional economic contractions such as the "lost decade" of the 1980s in Latin America; the 1990's post-socialist contraction in Central and Eastern Europe, Russia, Ukraine and former Soviet republics in the transition from central planning to market-based economies; the East Asian financial crises of 1996–1998 that hit South Korea, Indonesia, Thailand, Malaysia and the Philippines after a previous period of rapid surge in capital inflows from abroad and internal deregulation of their banking systems.

Recessions may have multiple origins: price corrections in financial markets after a phase of over-valued asset prices, excessive monetary creation followed by austerity policies to curb inflation, contractions in aggregate demand (consumption, investment, exports), the collapse in terms of trade (the ratio of export prices over import prices), sharp reversals in capital inflows (the so-called "sudden stops") and other factors.

These recessions are bound to affect the art market in various ways. Goetzmann et al. (2011) writing on "art and money" construct an index of real art prices for a period of near 250 years (1765–2007). The study shows a steady upward trend of art prices from the second third of the 18th century up to around 1870. Then prices turn very volatile coinciding with the "long depression" between 1883–1896 this was more a period of price deflation rather than a "traditional" depression entailing sharp declines in output, employment and investment. In the 20th century, art prices peaked in 1914 at the start of World War I, then in 1929 (the year of the stock market crash) followed by a decline in the 1930s (great depression), recovering in the early 1940s (coinciding with the onset of World War II) and reaching a new peak in 1973 followed by a bearish market in the rest of the 1970s. In the 1980s, art prices recovered reaching a peak in 1990. Then the study compares the evolution of an index of stock prices and art prices from 1830 to 2007. In general, both prices tend to *move together* (a positive correlation). In other words, both art prices and equities prices tend to follow the general ups and downs of the business cycle, but this correlation is not perfect with differences in the timing and intensity of the changes in art prices and stock prices across different economic cycles. After the worst part of the great depression (mid-1930s), the recovery of equity prices was more rapid than the resurgence of art prices. In contrast, in the stagflation of the 1970s equity prices suffered more than art prices particularly in the second half of the 1970s. In turn, the decline in equity prices at the end of the dot.com bubble in the early 2000s was stronger than art prices that recovered more swiftly.

5.3 Sensitivity of art prices to macroeconomic cycles

The historical experience of the art market (including the first two decades of the 21st century) shows a considerable sensitivity of the demand for art to macroeconomic cycles of expansion and contraction (see Chapter 6). The *aggregate* evidence suggests the art market tends to behave in a *pro-cyclical way*, with *total* sales/volumes rising in the upswings (phases of expansion of GDP, employment, investment), and declining in the downswings of the business cycle (growth slowdown, recessions). As shown in Table 5.1 and Figure 5.1, both sales and volumes fell sharply in 2009 at the bottom of the global financial crisis yet recovered rather forcefully in the first few years after the crisis (this recovery failed to be sustained a few years after 2012). Aggregate sales in the global market for art were U$62 billion in 2008, declining to U$39 billion in 2009, reaching near a decade later U$67 billion dollars in 2018.

The phase of a macroeconomic cycle can affect differently the various segments of the art market. While macroeconomic downturns and financial crashes probably hit (in 2008–2009) all segments of the art market the post-crisis recovery favoured, mostly, large auction houses and big galleries, with those in the middle-lower end segment of the market lagging behind. In fact, galleries with turnover in excess of U$50 million had yearly increases of over 10 percent in the post-2009 period, compared with declines in sales for dealers with sales less than U$1 million (McAndrew, 2018). Galleries with annual sales below U$250,000 did the worse in the market, confirming that the

Table 5.1 The global art market: Value and volume of transactions, 2008–2018

Year	Value (U$m)	Volume (m)
2008	62,020	43.7
2009	39,511	31
2010	57,025	35.1
2011	64,550	36.8
2012	56,698	35.5
2013	63,287	36.5
2014	68,237	38.8
2015	63,751	38.1
2016	56,948	36.1
2017	63,683	39
2018	67,380	39.8
Growth 2017–2018	6%	2%
Growth 2008–2018	9%	–9%

Source: Elaborated based on *art market 2019* public data.

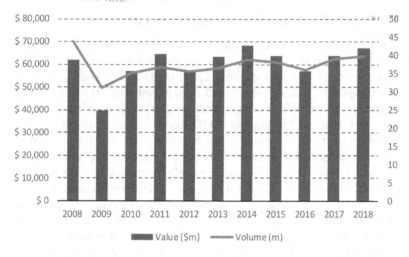

Figure 5.1 The global art market: Value and volume of transactions, 2008–2018.

Source: From Table 5.1.

post-global financial crisis recovery in the art market benefitted the high-end but not in equal way the rest of the market.[4]

5.4 War and conflict

A case of main social disruption is war. Armed conflicts entail the loss of human lives, the destruction of physical capital, buildings, property and provoke ecological damage. A few examples of war throughout history including the French-English war in the 18th century, the Napoleonic wars and the Crimean war in the 19th century, World War I and World War II in the 20th century besides a score of bilateral wars such as the Korean war in the early 1950s, the Vietnam war in the 1960s and early 1970s, the Gulf war and the Balkan in the early 1990s, the war in Libya in the 2010s and several other conflicts. Wars bring insecurity and uncertainty, and this has an impact on the art market although the effects on the demand for art and its prices are not always negative.

---

4 The high-end of the market concentrates a very thin segment of artists, while the remaining majority of them supply the middle-range and lower-end of the market through the segment of galleries, dealers and auction houses.

We can identify the following impacts of a situation of war and their aftermath on the art market:

1. Perhaps surprisingly, wars (and their aftermath) can also trigger *bursts of artistic creativity*: think of Picasso's Guernica during the Spanish civil war of 1936–1939 and the blossoming of abstract expressionism in America after World War II.
2. War can lead to the *looting* of art and cultural treasures in occupied countries (this practice affected private collections, public museums and collections of persecuted minorities in World War II).[5]
3. Art markets may offer a *safe haven* during wartime in terms of discretion, portability and protection from inflation.
4. The financing the war through measures of financial repression set artificially distorting equity and private bond prices to induce the acquisition of government war bonds can *boost* art prices through substitution effects in asset portfolios.
5. War-induced inflation and associated *monetary reforms* can affect (in positive or negative ways) the demand for artwork.

5.4.1 Art prices in World War I and World War II

In France, World War I was accompanied by stagnant art prices; in contrast, prices went up (increased) during World War II. A study of the evolution of art prices between July 1911 and July 1925 in France is David (2014).[6] The price data come from the registers of the *Gazette de l'Hotel Drouot*, the main art auction place in Paris and contains, mostly, the price of high-end impressionists and post-impressionist paintings.

The behaviour of art prices is compared with the price of competing assets such as stocks (CAC 40), government bonds (RENTE) and real estate for the same period (from July 1911 to July 1925). Before the war, say between 1911 and 1913 art prices increased but during the war period (1914–1917) they remained depressed as sales of paintings were at a minimum and the market came to a virtual standstill.

Immediately after the war, in 1918, there was a short price rebound, then fell again in 1919 and remained stagnant until 1924. Before the war, sales were dominated by masterpieces but during the war, and in 1918, impressionists and Fauvism apparently drove the market.

5 Nicholas (1995) provides an exhaustive account of the Nazi looting of art in Europe in WWII.
6 David (2014).

Prices of alternative assets such as real estate, bonds and stocks remained also depressed during World War I with real estate slowly recovering since 1921. In contrast, since 1920 gold prices went upward sharply. These price dynamics suggest that art could *not* be considered as having played the role of a safe-haven asset during World War I.[7] It was *gold* the asset that really played that role after the war.

The economic situation in France after World War I was complicated. The country had difficulties in enforcing war reparations from Germany sanctioned by the Treaty of Versailles. In addition, the French economy was incubating monetary and exchange rate disequilibria with the value of the franc fluctuating relative to foreign currencies and domestic prices behaving in an erratic way.

David (2014) shows that in the period 1911–1925 art *underperformed* stocks, bonds, real estate and gold if measured by the annualized rate of return. To incorporate risk in these comparisons the Sharpe index is used that computes the difference between the return of a given asset relative to a safe asset (for example a government bond) divided by the difference in the standard deviations of the returns between the two assets. The theory says a risk-averse investor will demand a higher return to compensate for tolerating greater volatility. In the French case for the period under analysis, the best performing assets are gold if measured by its annual rate of return and real estate if measured by the Sharpe ratio. Art performs poorly both in terms of average returns (negative) and had the lowest Sharpe ratio.

As said before, the dynamics of art prices differed substantially in World War II compared with World War I in France. In contrast with the slow dynamic of the art market in World War I, art prices *went up* sharply in 1941 after the German occupation when auctions resumed. Further price increases took place in 1942 and in 1943–1944.

Various effects seem to have operated to produce an *active* art market in a situation of military occupation by a foreign country. In fact, around 25,000 paintings, drawings and engravings were sold at the Hotel Dourout period between 1940 and 1944 during the occupation.[8]

A factor behind the art market stimulus in World War II was the high purchasing power of higher-rank German officials who were interested in acquiring art, a pattern also observed in Belgium and the Netherland, countries that were also occupied by the Germans. This did not happen to occur during World War I (Paris was not occupied).

7 The recovery in art prices *after* the war was also quite erratic.
8 Oosterlinck (2011).

In addition, the occupier's policy of looting local art collections showed up in the market as part of the stolen artwork was brought for sale contributing to activate art trade.

Another factor was the appearance of the so-called "nouveaux riches" (new rich) constituted by shopkeepers and parallel-market operators that made handsome profits by charging high prices at times of uncertainty and rationing. The "nouveaux riches" wanted assets whose markets were not intervened by the authorities and that could preserve their real value. Art – particularly landscapes and still lives – started to play that role, so the demand for artwork as a "secure" asset exerted an upward pressure on prices.

There is consensus among economic historians that art objects during war and occupation were convenient investments in terms of discretion, portability, tax shields, inflation-proof and lack of market intervention by the state.[9] Some of these dimensions could be shared by gold and foreign exchange but they often faced restrictions to be acquired in the legal market in wartime.

Also, the prevailing *monetary regimes and market regulations* differed between World War I and World War II. In France, in World War I, capital mobility abroad was not openly restricted. But in World War II there were tight capital controls in occupied countries with financial repression techniques inducing people to acquire government bonds as a way for governments to finance the occupation and war expenses. In fact, the French government placed several restrictions on the stock exchange market such as forced registration procedures and price caps (restricting price increases and/or establishing price ceilings). These restrictions reduced the effective real return of holding equity (net of transaction costs) prompting portfolio substitution away from equities toward art and gold.

An article, "The Price of Degenerate Art" (Oosterlinck, 2011) presents rates of return, standard deviation and Sharpe ratios for equity, gold (napoleon, gold-index), government bonds (RENTE), foreign exchange (British pounds, US dollars, Swiss francs) during the occupation period between 1941 and 1944 in Paris. The results show that the highest monthly rate of return corresponds to the art market followed by gold. Art investments have also the highest standard deviation (a measure of risk in the returns) but the highest Sharpe ratio corresponds to gold Napoleon (that had to be acquired in the black market) followed by art.

---

9 See Oosterlinck (2011) and David (2014).

The impact of the monetary reform (the Gutt Plan)[10] that took place in the aftermath of World War II on the Belgium art market has been studied by David and Oosterlinck (2015) using an art price database of 3,000 pieces sold between 1945 and 1951 that includes canvases [the dominant item], cardboards, etching, prints, sculptures, oils, watercolours, obtained from the *Giroux Gallery* the main art trader in Belgium at that time. The authors find that the art market crashed between 1944–1947 but experienced a rebound after and that the crash was probably associated with the reduction in the money supply due to the monetary reform.

Three factors can be advanced to explain the initial *decline* in art prices after the end of the hostilities of World War II (the liberation of Belgium took place in 1944) and the monetary reform:[11]

a   A *rebalancing of portfolios* with a fall in demand for art (a "safe" asset during war conditions) and a shift to more traditional financial assets such as stocks. The demand for stocks was bound to increase following the decline in uncertainty and the lifting of financial repression of the wartime period (some controls on nominal interest rates remained after the war).

b   The *prosecution of war collaborators* that profited from the occupation and acquired artwork to invest their liquidity surpluses may have led to a rush of selling in the market (a supply-side effect).

c   The effect of monetary reform that eliminated high-denomination bills and taxed real balances to get rid of *monetary overhangs*.[12] This amounted to a cut in liquid wealth inducing a reduction in the demand for artwork and an increase in its supply. In a situation of lack of liquidity, households will use available money to buy food and essentials.

---

10 Camille Gutt was the Finance Minister and architect of the monetary plan oriented to soak liquidity and prevent a surge of inflation a problem that occurred after World War I. The monetary plan, however, was not free of criticism due to the confiscation of money holdings from citizens.

11 David and Oosterlinck (2012).

12 A "money overhang" is defined as an excessive accumulation of cash balances – beyond what would be an optimal portfolio allocation – in conditions of price controls, rationing and monetary financing of fiscal deficits (all typical of war situations). Solimano (1991) offers various examples of monetary reforms after World War I and World War II in Central and Eastern Europe.

6 How the super-rich is shaping the art sector in an era of high inequality

With Paula Solimano

6.1 Introduction

This chapter examines the relationship between economic elites, inequality of wealth (and income), the transnational capitalist class and the art market. Economic elites can be defined in terms of wealth and income although they have symbolic traits that go beyond purely economic considerations. An empirical definition of economic elites is the group that represents the top 1 percent (or the top 0.1 percent) of the income and wealth distribution of a country. Capitalist elites can be defined in functional terms as owners of productive wealth and a group that sets the rules for capital accumulation, current production and control the labour process. Elites accumulate financial and non-financial assets including artworks. As discussed in Chapter 4 *art accumulation* may be based on aesthetic grounds, can be a signal of status or a financial investment.

The top art collectors in the private sector belong to the global elites and are concentrated in a few cities and tend to obtain their incomes in the most dynamic sectors of the current capitalist economy. The three biggest art collecting cities are New York, London and São Paulo, (the home to more than half of Latin American art collectors) Miami, Los Angeles, Paris, Berlin and Hong Kong. These cities concentrate a high proportion of artists, art dealers, galleries and host satellite fairs and biennials. The sources of wealth of these collectors are largely finance, real estate, construction and retail, followed by extractive industries, media and advertising. Inheritance could be another important source, although an analysis of the billionaires list of Forbes Magazine shows that "self-made billionaires" (whose wealth is not inherited) comprise an important proportion of the total number of billionaires of several countries.[1]

1 Freund (2016).

DOI: 10.4324/9781003215127-6

The growing ownership of artwork of high value by private collectors and wealthy families has several implications for the relative position of the art market in society. Nowadays private collectors have an active participation on boards of museums and other non-profit organizations to which they lend and/or donate pieces from their collections and contribute with funding. Their presence in art institutions at a moment when public funding in art is shrinking affects the balance between the private and public domains in the art sector. As shown in chapter 2, the art market has become quite international in scope with three countries dominating the scene: The United States, Great Britain and China. This is accompanied by a growing mobility of talent in the cultural sector due to the benefits of concentration of artists in large cities with a large number of museums, art schools, critics, galleries, auction houses and purchasing power (Addison, 2008).

6.2 The withdrawal of the state in the cultural sector

As the state, during the neoliberal age, tends to withdraw support activities to cultural institutions, it follows a shrinking of public funding for art leading to more injection of private resources to art institutions. Funding is channelled into the field of visual art through the purchase of artworks and the sponsorship of art institutions, among other initiatives. This pattern of substituting private funding for public funding is in line with the growing marketization and privatization of a host of cultural activities in the neoliberal phase of global capitalism, a practice that certainly includes the art sector.

It can be argued that the scarcity of public funding for art, and the boom of single-collector museums (private institutions) potentially pose a threat to the very existence and/or the financial health of public museums, as their ability to acquire works of art, build, remodel and expand their exhibition spaces and organize and host large-scale shows depends, largely, on the priorities of private donors and their charitable contributions of money and artworks. This dependence is due to several reasons: one is them is the fact that historically important objects have reached extravagant prices at auctions, where works of art are "flipped" (purchased and sold in a short time frame) to earn a quick profit. The individuals involved in these practices are often those who then contribute to the institutions at stake.

The rise of art prices also pushes up the costs of security, maintenance and insurance of art collections. These costs can become increasingly burdensome to large museums in advanced economies and developing countries. Other significant costs are related to property and rent, which are continually rising in the key cities of the art industry. However, as shown by the *2014 Art Collector Report*, in the United States alone, 53 percent of the top collectors are involved with public museums, and over 90 percent of art collections held in public trust by American museums have been donated by private individuals, which indicates that the growing presence of private institutions does not necessarily lead to a demise of museums – at least not among the internationally revered institutions.[2] Yet what is perhaps more worrisome is the fact that the bulk of these donations, in terms of value, is directed to large museums, such as New York's MoMA, the Metropolitan Museum of Art and Guggenheim Museum, rather than those located in poor, rural and/or overlooked areas. In fact, more than half of the contributed income in 2009 – individual or corporate gifts and grants – went to 2 percent of arts organizations, which had budgets over U$10 million.[3]

As public funding becomes less available, and smaller institutions have little or no access to wealthy donors, they are bound to face less resources and less attention by the public and media, as their modest initiatives are met with extravagant exhibitions at renowned museums and galleries. One can only wonder how this affects their ability to attract visitors and, on a larger scale, tourists, and, more importantly, their possibility of participating in the creation and narration of collective identity. The MoMA in New York has the largest number of members of the Forbes 400 list of all the corporations and non-profit organizations worldwide, beating rich companies such as Google and Facebook.[4] As we ask what motivates these wealthy individuals to donate to the arts, we must also remember that their donations are not only directed to this sector. The whereabouts of these donations, in fact, don't always align with the political agendas of the cultural institutions in which they are involved. This can be observed in the political parties and candidates to which rich donors contribute.

Fraser's *Museums, Money, and Politics* (2016), shows that 70 percent of total political contributions from museum donors of the Museum of Contemporary Art, Los Angeles were directed to Republican/Conservative Parties in the United States. Similarly, more than 65 percent of reported political contributions by board members of the Whitney Museum of American Art went to the same parties (Frazer,

2 Bossier et al. (2014).
3 Horwitz (2016).
4 Kroll (2015).

2016). This suggests for the United States a somewhat contradictory relation between arts giving and political interests, as it could be expected that supporting museums with progressive agendas would go hand-in-hand with supporting progressive political groups.

Concerning art institutions, billionaires through donations of money and artworks get influential positions in advisory boards and committees, shaping the agenda, mission and values of the world's most important museums. They make decisions regarding acquisitions and exhibition programs, impacting directly the work of curators, researchers, archivists and art-handlers, and are given the opportunity of showcasing their works in the most-visited shows (including their names in the provenance of such pieces). This exposure ultimately raises the symbolic and financial value of their entire collections. Additionally, these philanthropic endeavours provide the transnational capitalist class with access to a global cultural elite that attends biennials, art fairs and major exhibitions, and thereby gives them status, symbolic capital along with the opportunity to create and nurture a philanthropic, arts-loving image.

This strong involvement in art institutions – either private or public – also leads collectors to enjoy special tax treatments, which is an important incentive to consider. Tax breaks are given according to the financial value of their donations, which are backed up by experts and appraisers. These may be art historians, dealers, conservators or others, who possess a broad knowledge of the art market, and the standards, principles and methodologies that surround art pieces. Incentivizing collectors to donate artworks to public museums, some institutions have inflated the prices of artworks in order to facilitate them with larger tax deductions.[5]

6.3   Hiding art in the shadows: The emergence of freeports

Top collectors are increasingly using artwork as investments to reduce their tax burden. More worrisome perhaps, is the fact that some participants use the art market to launder money obtained from illicit activities such as drug dealing and informal arms trade (see chapter 4).[6]

---

5 Such was the case of Jiri Frel, the Getty Museum's former curator of Greek and Roman art, who helped donors obtain high appraisals on gifts made to the antiquities department. This would translate into higher tax deductions. For more on Mr. Frel, see *The New York Times*, 1987, "The Getty Reports a Scandal".
6 Adam (2014).

A mechanism to keep valuable artwork outside the public domain and protected from taxation is *freeports*. These are sophisticated physical facilities storing valuable paintings, sculptures, printings and so on besides other luxury items such as expensive cars, wine, gold and diamonds. Furthermore, *freeports* are storages outside of the territorial jurisdiction of any country.

Historically, freeports arose as tax-free facilities in ports used for storing goods while the merchandise was in transit to other destinations, the reason for which "custom authorities [allowed] duties and taxes to be suspended until goods [reached] their final destination"[7]. Now the merchandise "in transit" is artwork that may be stored a long time (several years) waiting for its price to increase.

There are high-tech freeports in Geneva, Zurich, Luxembourg, Monaco, Singapore and Beijing in which art and collectibles increase in value while in storage.[8] As long as fees are paid no serious restrictions are put on who may use them, from individuals to business entities, benefiting both from the tax-suspension system. While not all taxes are exempted in these facilities, value-added taxes are, as well as sales taxes, which are crucial considering that some pieces of fine art, including high-value artists, such as Amedeo Modigliani, Vincent Van Gogh and Paul Cézanne. The other side of this practice is that national states see part of their tax revenues eroded.

The geographic location of freeports for artworks and luxuries (watches, wine, expensive cars and private airplanes) often coincide with the locations of tax havens for outside bank deposits as is the case of Switzerland, Luxembourg and Singapore, among others. A true industry of asset protection catered to the very rich is developed in which highly valuable physical objects are subject to museum-like standards. Pieces are held in custody under high-security standards with transactions and protocols taking place largely hidden from the general public.

6.4 The rise of the super-rich: Wealth concentration and inequality

The evidence shows the growth of the art market (particularly its upper segment) and the concentration of wealth at the top tend to go together (see Figure 6.1, Table 6.1 and Figure 6.2). Global capitalism

7 Solimano and Solimano (2020).
8 Solimano (2018a, 2018b).

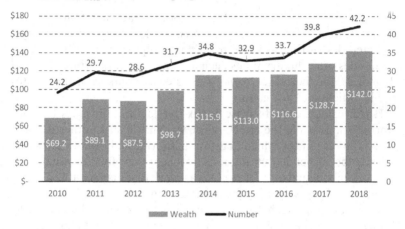

Figure 6.1 Number (Trillion) and wealth of dollar millionaires (Million) 2010–2018.

Source: Elaborated on data from art market 2019.

in recent decades has seen a rapid increase in the number and value of assets of wealthy people (from millionaires to billionaires). As shown in Figure 6.1 from 2010 to 2018, the number of millionaires (individuals with net worth above U$1 million) has increased From 24.2 million to 42.2 million and their assets have grown from $69.2 trillion to $142 trillion, respectively, almost doubling over a period of 9 years.

The top importance of the US art market is related, among other things, with the fact that the United States concentrates the largest number of millionaires in the world (43 percent of the world's high net worth individuals – HNWIs), ultra-millionaires (49 percent of global ultra-HNWI) and billionaires, (32 percent of them), see Table 6.1 for 2017. In turn, China comes third in the world in terms of millionaires (6 percent) and second in terms of ultra-HNWIs (13 percent) and billionaires (26 percent), showing the formation of a powerful wealthy elite in China with very high high-purchasing power that is increasingly devoted, at least in part, to the acquisition of artwork.

Regarding indicators of within-country concentration of wealth, the data shows, since the 1980s, at the start of the neoliberal era, a significant increase in the wealth share of the top 1 percent has taken place in the United States of America, followed since the 1990s in China, Russia a trend that has been more moderate in France and the UK. The evolution of wealth inequality in main capitalist economies in the 20th century followed a U-shape: there was first a decline in the

Table 6.1 Global share of millionaires (HNWIs), ultra-millionaires (ultra-HNWIs) and billionaires in total personal wealth (percent, 2017)

HNWIs (wealth above U$1m)		Ultra-HNWIs (wealth above U$50m)		Global share of dollar billionaires in 2017	
	Share (percent)		Share (percent)		Share (percent)
United States	43	United States	49	United States	32
Japan	8	China	13	China	26
China	6	Germany	5	Germany	4
Italy	4	United Kingdom	3	Russia	3
France	5	France	2	Sweden	2
United Kingdom	6	Australia	2	United Kingdom	2
Germany	5	Canada	2	Switzerland	2
Canada	3	Switzerland	2	India	2
Australia	3	Italy	2	Turkey	2
Korea	2	Japan	1	Canada	1
Others	16	Others	19	Others	24
Total	100	Total	100	Total	100

Source: Elaborated on data from McAndrew (2018) and Credit Suisse (2017a, 2017b).

concentration of wealth at the top between the 1910s and the 1960s, followed since the 1980s by higher wealth concentration at the top of the distribution in these economies following the onset of the neoliberal era.[9]

Historical research investigating the impact of wealth inequality, stock prices and the art market focussing on the British art market from 1905 to 2007. Goetzmann et al. (2011) found a positive correlation between wealth (and income) inequality and art prices, a relation that

9 Around 1913 in the United States, United Kingdom and France the wealth's share of the top 1 percent was in the range 45–65 percent, declining, over time, to reach to 20–30 percent in the 1970s to increase afterwards coinciding with the onset of globalization and neoliberalism. Since then, the top 1 percent wealth's share in the United States of America roughly doubled from around 20 percent in the late 1970s to near 40 percent in 2013. In the United Kingdom, since the Thatcher conservative government, the wealth's share of the top 1 percent also increased (stabilizing at around 20 percent in the period 1980–2015), reversing its previous downward trend registered since World War I until the 1970s. In France, the top wealth share experienced a rapid surge in the mid-1990s to decline afterwards, stabilizing at a higher level than its historical record of the 1970s and 1980s. See Solimano (2018a, 2018b).

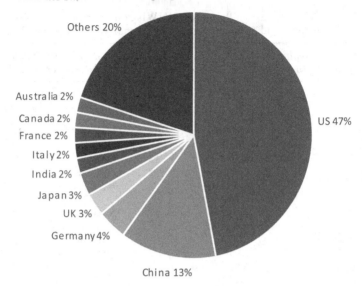

Figure 6.2 Global share of millionaires wealth more than $50 million, 2018.

Source: Elaborated from data of art market 2019.

becomes stronger since the 1970s when wealth inequality markedly increases in Anglo-Saxon countries.[10] The authors conclude that in periods of increased wealth inequality we should expect a boom in the art market as liquid wealth holders invest more strongly in artwork. A boom of such characteristics was observed in the years preceding the global financial crisis of 2008–2009 (Chapter 6). The rise in inequality in the United States spanning over four decades – from Reagan to Trump –[11] is also associated with the expansion of its very large internal art market.

We can distinguish several channels through which wealth concentration at the top (upper 1 percent or top 0.1 percent) affects the working of the art market:

a   At times of recession and/or financial crisis, asset prices and the value of aggregate wealth tend to be reduced, affecting the demand for art. We may call this a generally negative "wealth effect". An exception, though, to this pattern is the recession of COVID -19 in

10 Goetzmann et al.
11 Taylor (2020).

2020 and 2021 in which the value of financial wealth has *increased* sharply due to rising asset prices particularly after main central banks adopted policies of quantitative easing.

b   Conversely, in upturns and booms, there is a rise in stock prices and property prices increasing the value of financial wealth. A certain fraction of the increase in the value of wealth is spent on artwork and luxury goods.

c   A rise in uncertainty can be expected to increase the demand for art as a way to diversify wealth portfolios.

d   The demand for masterpieces and highly valued artists (Da Vinci, Monet, Van Gogh, Koons, Picasso, Modigliani and others) may be largely insensitive (inelastic) to short-run macroeconomic fluctuations.

e   A high degree of wealth concentration at the top is often accompanied by the creation of a niche market of large galleries and big-internationalized auction houses oriented to serve rich collectors. Empirically, the demand for expensive artwork seems to be highly correlated with the number and stock of wealth of millionaires and billionaires.

7 Investing in art as protection against economic turbulence
Prices in the cycle 1998–2018

7.1 Introduction

Continuing with the question of how macroeconomic fluctuations and cycles of boom and bust in economic activity affect the art market in this chapter we investigate the behaviour of *art prices* (taken from Artprice.com) in the period 1998–2018. These two decades have been rich in macro-financial cycles and economic (and political) events with lasting global impacts affecting advanced economies and the global economy at large. A list of features and events of these two decades are:

a   Continued economic interdependence across nations (globalization) although with some important reversals such as Brexit and the trade wars between the United States and China.
b   The incubation of asset price bubbles in hi-tech stocks in the late 1990s and the real estate sector in the United States, United Kingdom, Spain, Australia and other countries between 2003 and 2007. At some point, these bubbles prickled generating downturns and crashes.
c   Augmented financial fragility and growing indebtedness by households, governments and corporations.
d   The development, in some main economies, of macroeconomic imbalances such as fiscal deficits and fragile balance of payments positions.[1]

---

1 Mainstream macroeconomics, highly influential in central banks and ministries of finance, argued that in the 1990s and 2000s we were living in a "great moderation" of low inflation and steady GDP growth. This optimistic assessment has been criticized since it disregarded problems of financial fragility and large swings in asset prices that can be destabilizing.

DOI: 10.4324/9781003215127-7

e   A rise in personal income and wealth inequality, particularly in the
United States, United Kingdom, China, Russia and other countries.
f   Increased international mobility of educated individuals for purposes of study and work.

In this context, the size and global reach of the art market expanded
considerably across different countries.[2] The art price indices used
in this chapter are weighted averages of the price of paintings, sculptures, prints, photos and artefacts.[3] They are computed globally and
also for main national art markets in the United States, Europe and
Asia and expressed in real US dollars and real euros on a quarterly
basis for the period 1998–2018.

The chapter explores the correlation between art prices and stock
prices, gold prices, oil prices and bitcoin prices (the main cryptocurrency). These are alternative assets that compete with artwork in personal portfolios.

As shown in previous chapters, stock prices are highly *pro-cyclical*,
rising in upturns and falling in downturns while gold prices tend to be
counter-cyclical exhibiting safe-haven features that make the comparison with art prices interesting and relevant. Oil may be pro-cyclical as
well. In contrast, bitcoin prices defy simple business cycle correlations
(Solimano, 2018c).

7.2 The 1998 to 2018 period

We can distinguish four phases in this period for the global art price
index expressed in US dollars (U$):

i   A decade-long boom between 1998 (Q1) to 2008 (Q1), before the
onset of the global financial crisis.
ii   A sharp price correction in 2008–2009.
iii A strong but relatively short rebound in 2009–2011 and
iv   A new correction, followed by ups and downs through 2018 (see
Table 7.1).

2 The recovery in stock prices after the crisis of 2008–2009 was quite impressive in
the USA and was followed also by rises in housing prices. China (the second/third
art market) also experienced very rapid economic growth with high inequality in
the 1998–2018 period.
3 The prices are from reported transactions by auction houses (deducted their premiums). They may not necessarily reflect the reality of the *whole* art market that
includes also transactions carried out by smaller galleries.

Table 7.1 Global real art price index, 1998–2018 (in US$, base 2015 (Q4) = 100, deflated by US CPI)

Pre-crisis increase (T/P)	Change, percent
1998 (Q1) – 2008 (Q1)	64.6
Crisis correction (P/T)	
2008 (Q1) – 2009 (Q4)	−39.6
Recovery/Boom (T/P)	
2009 (Q4) – 2011 (Q3)	77.0
New correction (P/T)	
2011 (Q3) – 2018 (Q4)	−53.0

Note:
CPI = Consumer Price Index, T = Trough, P = Peak. Elaboration of series from Artprice.com.

In general, art prices followed the general cycles of economic activity and financial cycles in the sense of appreciating in the booming years, (before the downturn of 2008–2009), falling sharply during the crisis (2008–2009) and recovering afterwards, although that recovery was erratic and volatile.

The cycle in stock market prices (Standard & Poor 500) differed in *intensity* from the cycle of art prices (Table 7.2). The increase in S&P500 *before* the crisis was relatively modest compared with the appreciation in art prices. In fact, between 1998 and 2007 the S&P 500 index increased by 14 percent (trough to peak) compared with the 65 percent increase in the US$ art price index over a similar period. In turn, at the time of the crash, the S&P500 experienced a decline, in real terms, of 47 percent between 2007 (Q3) and 2009 (Q1). Then *after* the crisis, there was a very strong and protracted rebound in stock prices: an increase of near 200 percent in the real S&P 500 index from the bottom of the crisis in 2009 (Q1) and 2018 (Q4), Table 7.2. The relatively steady upward trajectory of the S&P 500 in the post-2008–2009 crisis decade contrasts with the more volatile behaviour in global art prices over the same period.

Table 7.2 Real stock market prices (S&P 500), 1998–2018 (2015 (Q4) = 100, deflated by US CPI)

Pre-crisis increase (T/P)	Change, percent
1998 (Q1) – 2007 (Q3)	14.2
Crisis correction (P/T)	
2007 (Q3) – 2009 (Q1)	−47.0
Post-crisis recovery/boom (T/P)	
2009 (Q1) – 2018 (Q3)	197.0

Table 7.3 Real gold prices, 2001–2018 (2015 (Q4) = 100, deflated by US CPI)

Upward cycle (T/P)	Change, percent
2001 (Q3) – 2011 (Q3)	401.0
Correction (P/T)	
2011 (Q3) – 2015 (Q4)	−61.0
Recovery (T/P)	
2015 (Q4) – 2018 (Q3)	3.5

In turn, gold prices experienced a long upward cycle of 11 years – between 2001 and 2011 – entailing a 400 percent increase in real terms in that period. Interestingly, and in line with the hypothesis that gold is a truly counter-cyclical/safe-haven asset, there was *no decline* in gold prices in 2008–2009. A correction in gold prices, however, took place *after four years* of the irruption of the global financial crisis and was sharp: a drop of 61 percent – between 2011 and 2015 – in the real price of gold followed later by a slight increase of 3.5 percent between 2015 and 2018 (Table 7.3).

Figure 7.1 presents global average art prices in US dollars and Euros compared with gold prices and Standard and Poor. In turn, the evolution of average art prices in the markets of the United States, United Kingdom and France is shown in Figure 7.2. The chart depicts

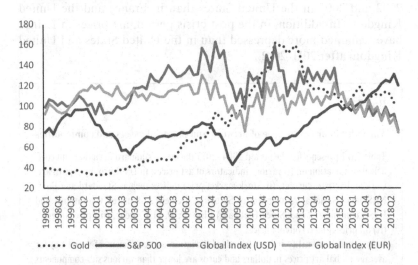

Figure 7.1 Quarterly real global prices of art, assets and commodities: S&P 500, gold and art price (real prices, 2015 (Q4) = 100, 1998 (Q1) to 2018 (Q4)).

Source: Own Elaboration Artprice.com, Pink sheet (World Bank) and Yahoo Finance.

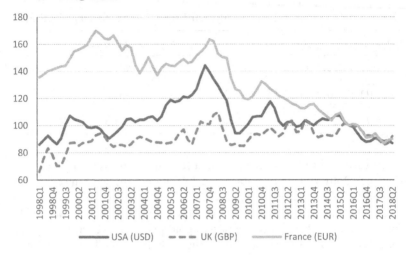

Figure 7.2 Quarterly real art market prices by country: United States, United Kingdom and France (1998 (Q1) – 2018 (Q2), base 2015 (Q4) = 100, deflated by domestic CPI).

Source: Artprice.com.

differences in intensity and duration of the pre-crisis boom among the three national art markets with sharper increases in prices between 2002 and 2007 in the United States than in France and the United Kingdom. In addition, in the post-crisis period, art prices in France have remained more depressed than in the United States and United Kingdom after 2011–2012.

Box 7.1

Volatility in prices by type of artwork and financial assets and commodities

Table 7.B.1 presents for the period 2004–2015 the mean, standard deviation and coefficient of variation of: (i) various indicators of art prices: in US, Euro, by type of artwork and artistic current, (ii) stock market price indices such as Standard and Poor, NASDAQ (National Association of Securities Dealers Automated Quotations) and FTSE (Financial Times Stock Exchange) China A50, MSC index, (iii) price of gold, (iv) oil prices and (v) bitcoin prices.

In general, volatility indices (standard deviation and coefficient of variation) for average global art prices in dollars and euros are lower than various sub-components (particularly for price indices of paintings and contemporary artwork). Items with high price volatility are the NASDAQ composite and FTSE China A50 and oil prices. Particularly high is the volatility of bitcoin prices (see Solimano, 2018c).

Table 7.B.1 Volatility in real prices of art assets and commodities (fourth quarter of 2004 to second quarter of 2018, real prices, base 2015 (Q4) = 100)

	Mean	*Standard deviation*	*Coef. of variation*
Real art price global index (U$)	125.36	19.48	0.16
Real art price global index (EUR)	108.43	12.24	0.11
Paintings	132.88	28.93	0.22
Prints	119.90	18.77	0.16
Sculptures	126.42	24.48	0.19
Photographs	114.39	20.29	0.18
Drawings	107.15	22.56	0.21
Old masters	150.08	39.14	0.26
19th century	135.99	41.82	0.31
Modern	143.10	34.34	0.24
Post-war	117.91	18.43	0.16
Contemporary	133.17	23.54	0.18
United States (U$)	107.27	13.83	0.13
United Kingdom (GBP)	94.13	6.10	0.06
France (EUR)	122.93	21.58	0.18
NASDAQ composite	71.87	27.02	0.38
Nikkei 225	80.70	21.37	0.26
S&P 500	80.93	20.07	0.25
Gold	104.31	31.33	0.30
Oil	188.28	59.78	0.32
FTSE China A50	130.50	42.50	0.33
MSCI world historical data	91.26	15.14	0.17
Bitcoin*	350.32	744.51	2.13
Average (without bitcoin)	117.59	25.58	0.22
Average	127.71	56.84	0.30

Source: Own elaboration.

* Data from 2010 (Q3).

Source: Federal reserve economic data, Yahoo Finance, Investing.com, CoinDesk.com, Pink sheet from World Bank and Artprice.com.

7.3 Is art a safe-haven asset? A comparison with gold and other assets

The empirical evidence for the art market in the period 1998–2018 shows that *average* art prices behaved in a *pro-cyclical* way during the cycle preceding and following the global financial crisis of 2008–2009. Of course, as discussed before some individual items of famous artists – masterpieces and contemporary art pieces – may *not* be affected by downturns and recessions and their prices even *increase in bad times.* Our evidence is based on aggregate price indices; of course, the behaviour of individual artwork prices may have shown different patterns during the last 20-year cycle, therefore the diversification could have taken place through specific art pieces of different art schools and artists.

To explore further the issue of safe-haven assets during main downturns, we look at the behaviour of gold prices during three historical episodes of recession/slumps of the last 90 years and then we will present correlations between art prices and the price of other assets.

7.3.1 Evidence I: The behaviour of real gold prices in three main slumps

As shown in Table 7.4 real gold prices *increased* in the Great Depression of the 1930s, the stagflation of the 1970s and the global financial crisis of 2008–2009, the three main global crises of the last 90 years (before COVID-19). Examining the first episode, while real gold prices increased by around 20 percent in the decade *before* the Great Depression (period 1920–1929, see Table 7.4) *during* the Great Depression gold prices *surged* from 282 dollars per ounce in

Table 7.4 Real gold price in three slumps (US per ounce deflated by US CPI, ratio peak/trough and percentage change)

	Real price (US per ounce)	Ratio peak/trough and percent change
	Great Depression of the 1930s	
1920 (6)	235.15	
1929 (9)	281.23	1.19 (19%)
1929 (12)	282.87	
1934 (2)	617.93	2.18 (118%)
	Stagflation of the 1970s	
1970 (12)	215.7	
1980 (1)	2,046.0	9.48 (848%)
	Global Financial Crisis of 2008–2009	
2001 (3)	350.5	
2005 (8)	523.58	
2008 (3)	1,064.96	
2011 (8)	1,891.60	
2014 (11)	1,176.04	5.39 (440%)

Source: Own elaboration based on Solimano (2017) and the London Bullion Market Association.

1929 (12) to 618 dollars per ounce in 1934 (3) representing an increase of 118 percent, not a bad investment for a depression period.

The stagflation of the 1970s that affected mostly advanced economies is another historical episode to test the demand for gold as a safe asset. The decade of the 1970s was accompanied by an acceleration of inflation following two main oil price shocks, slower economic growth, monetary and exchange rate instability along with geopolitical events such as the Vietnam war, terrorism in Europe and the Iran crisis of 1979. As shown in Table 7.4, there was an 850 percent increase in the real price of gold between the trough of 1970 (12) and the peak of 1980 (1), again a highly profitable investment for such a turbulent decade.

The third episode was the global financial crisis of 2008–2009 the first quasi-global crisis of the 21st century. The price of gold was at U$350 per ounce in 2001(3) and increased to U$1064.96 in 2008 (3), reaching a peak of U$1,891.6 in 2011 (8). The cumulative increase between the low of 2001(3) and the high of 2011 (8) was near 450 percent.

This combined evidence points that gold did, indeed, behave as a *counter-cyclical asset* in the three main slumps (Great Depression, stagflation and global financial crisis), playing the role of an effective hedge against economic turbulence and crises. It preserved and increased its value when other assets experienced economic losses. From the viewpoint of an individual investor, adding gold to a portfolio holding traditional financial assets delivered a degree of diversification (gold reduced the overall value-variance of a portfolio holding financial assets and art).

Another way to see this is by looking at the ratio between gold prices and stock market prices (S&P 500) over a long period of time, say the century running from 1914 to 2014. From Figure 7.3 it is clear that the ratio *increased in recessions and periods of economic volatility and uncertainty* (the early 1930s, the 1970s and 2008–2009 and other milder recessions) and *fell in periods of economic expansion and relative stability* such as the post-World War II expansion up to the 1960s (the golden age of capitalism period) and the long bull stock market that took place between the mid-1980s up to the late 1990s (high time of the neoliberal capitalism phase).

7.3.2 Evidence II: Price correlations

Another way to explore the potential for artwork to become a safe-haven asset is through a matrix of correlation between global art prices and various stock market price indices, gold, oil and

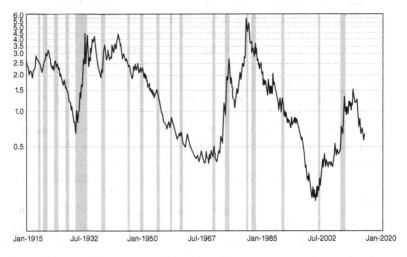

Figure 7.3 Ratio of the price of gold to stock market prices (S&P 500), 1915–2014.

Source: From data in Solimano (2017).

bitcoin (Table 7.5). The evidence is not entirely conclusive for all indices, but we can detect a *negative correlation* (statistically significant at 99 percent) between the real global art price index in U$ and two stock market indices: the real Nikkei 225 (−0.33) and the real S&P 500 (−0.37). In addition, the correlation with the MCSI index is also negative and significant but the value of the coefficient is small. At the same time, the global art market price index (in U$) has a *positive correlation with gold prices* (significant at 99 percent). As gold is clearly a safe-haven asset, art prices in dollars by being positively correlated with gold may share this feature of counter-cyclicality. However, the art price index in euros shows a negative correlation with gold (significant at 95 percent). Thus, correlation indices between gold and art may tell a somewhat different story regarding pro-cyclicality and safe-havens from the story that arises from looking at the co-movements between art market sales/prices and the cycles of Gross Domestic Product.[4]

4 The art price index in Euros is also negatively correlated with S& P 500 but the correlation with Nikkei 225 is very small (both are statistical insignificant). In turn, the correlation between art prices in Euros and gold is negative.

Table 7.5 Correlation matrix between art prices, financial assets and commodities (real prices, first quarter of 1998 to second quarter of 2018)

	Nikkei 225	S&P 500	Gold	Oil	Art price global index (U$)	Art price global index (EUR)	FTSE China A50[a]	MSCI world historical data[a]	Bitcoin[b]
Nikkei 225	1								
S&P 500	0.71 ***	1							
Gold	−0.44 ***	0.1	1						
Oil	−0.5 ***	−0.19 *	0.74 ***	1					
Art price global index (U$)	−0.33 ***	−0.37 ***	0.29 ***	0.7 ***	1				
Art price global index (EUR)	−0.01	−0.15	−0.24 **	0.1	0.54 ***	1			
FTSE China A50[a]	0.14	−0.04	0.04	0.21	0.19	0.19	1		
MSCI World historical Data[a]	0.88 ***	0.91 ***	−0.14	−0.24 *	−0.24 *	0.09	0.1	1	
Bitcoin[b]	0.59 ***	0.68 ***	−0.3 *	−0.33 *	−0.11	−0.51 ***	−0.54 ***	0.69 ***	1

Significance (99%) *** $p < 0.01$, significance (95%) ** $p < 0.05$, significance 90% * $(p < 0.1)$.

[a] Correlation are calculated from 2004 (Q4).
[b] Correlations are calculated from 2010 (Q3).

Finally, the correlation between the global art price indices in U$ and Euro with oil prices is negative and the correlation with the China stock market index is positive but not large. The correlation for the art price index in both U$ and Euro with bitcoin prices is negative and relatively sizable. This could reflect some competition between artwork and bitcoin in investor's portfolio.

8 Synthesis and public policy issues

Historically, the development of art markets was associated with the development of capitalism. In the Renaissance period, the cities of Florence, Venice, Genoa then Amsterdam and London became important art centres coinciding with their role in production, trade and centres of attraction of capital. In the 19th century, Paris became probably the most important art centre in the world and in the second half of the 20th century, this role shifted to New York reflecting the global economic hegemony of the United States. In turn, in the first two decades of the 21st century, China has irrupted as an important global player in the art market coming in volumes of sales after the United States and alternating with the UK. Again, this coincides with the rising global importance of the Chinese economy.

The evolution of the art market is clearly stimulated by waves of material prosperity and levels of economic development and the configuration of global economic powers. In turn, economic crises, and relative slowdowns in the rhythm of economic development that alters the global importance of countries is also reflected in the art market. Japan in the 1970s and 1980s was the most important art market in Asia but as the country entered a protracted period of economic stagnation in the 1990s, it lost its relative hegemony in the art sector being displaced by China.

The situation of the art market at the time of war shows the complex interaction of various factors. For example, during World War II there was an active trading in art with rising prices in occupied countries such as France, Netherlands and Belgium. Buying art was convenient for store owners and black-market traders in occupied Paris, Amsterdam and Brussels. These economic agents had accumulated liquidity and earned good profits trading in rationed markets. In a context of "financial repression" with government imposing caps on interest rates and stock prices and prohibitions to buy foreign

DOI: 10.4324/9781003215127-8

exchange for capital movements, artworks became a convenient way to hold wealth.

In contrast, holding stocks, gold, foreign exchange and real estate faced much more difficulties. Much of the attraction of holding art was related to conveniences such as discretion, liquidity, portability, inflation-proof and regulations affecting financial markets such as financial repression (special registration and ceiling on stock prices) oriented to induce investors to buy government bonds to finance the war effort.

In European countries occupied by the Nazi, art stayed largely unregulated and could be transported without too much hazards. In turn, Nazi officials participated in art markets through the selling of artwork looted from collectors and Jewish families.

During World War I, the art market in Paris was very depressed, affected by a sharp decline in the volume of trade and stagnant prices.

The process of artistic creativity is also sensitive to social change, revolution and war. The Mexican and Russian revolutions of the early 20th century triggered new currents – "conceptual revolutions" – such as muralism, constructivism, futurism, suprematism and other artistic currents whose permanence varied across time and space. In line with the purposes of democratizing the access to art, it was brought closer to the people in public buildings, streets, parks and not enclosed only in museums. Nonetheless, the post-revolution new energies and artistic freedom eventually fell of official grace as the USSR turned to Stalinism and Socialist Realism. In Mexico, the more conservative turn of government into a largely one-party state since the 1940s also had an adverse impact on the muralist movement.

The disarray and confusion of war also prompted new "conceptual revolutions" in art. World War I, for example, was followed by the rise of surrealism and forms of artistic expression that departed from previously accepted canons. In turn, World War II led to the rise of abstract expressionism in America helped by the immigration of innovative and experimentalist artists coming from Europe flying persecution and armed conflict in their home/residency countries. Later on, the consumption society of the 1950s and 1960s and the cult for material prosperity, particularly in the United States, triggered the appearance of pop art represented by Warhol, Lichtenstein and others.

Episodes of rapid democratization and progressive social transformation in Spain in 1933–1936, Bolivia 1952–1954, Chile 1970–1973, often reversed by military coups or counter-revolutionary armed insurrections, adopted different variants of large-scale paintings and muralism around themes directly related to the ongoing socio-political processes underway in these countries.

As of the early decades of the 21st century, the art sector reflects, in important ways, features of global capitalism and neoliberalism such as a tendency to commodification (transforming any object and activity into a commercial commodity), financialization (the increasing dependence on credit to buy things), high wealth inequality concentrated in small economic elites with ample purchasing power and influence on political and cultural institutions, industry-concentration and market polarization. Currently, a small number of auction houses and art dealers – catering for the upper end of the art sector – connected with art funds, family offices, commercial banks and hedge funds specialized in investment in artwork manage the trading of high-value pieces directed to very affluent customers. This upper end accounts for the bulk of sales in value terms but registers, in relative terms, a much lower number of transactions than the medium-size and small galleries. Moreover, the contribution of top-end galleries and auction houses to employment generation in the art sector is small. In fact, it is the segment of middle and small-size galleries that generate most of the employment in the art sector. Nonetheless, this middle segment is shrinking due to its structural limitations to compete with the ample resources and capacities of the upper segment of the art market.

New technologies are having an impact on the art market and finance. For example, sales by the internet and financial innovation such as new techniques of collateralization and securitization are being used in the art trade. The irruption of the blockchain with encrypted transactions and "Non-Fungible Tokens" potentially provides a way-out to the perennial problems of authentication in a market in which forgery, theft and faking are common practices.

The answer to the question of how to value art is not straightforward. The pricing of art is a complex endeavour somewhat similar to the pricing of long-lived assets such as physical capital or property. A difference, however, is that art does not carry a defined "fundamental value", which in the case of capital is the present value of future profits and in the case of property is the present value of future rental incomes. In spite of this, apparently neat price definitions of the value of capital and the value of property are not unaffected by inescapable uncertainty on a future that, by definition, is unknown making the valuation of these long-lived assets also a tricky process.

In the case of art, the piece can be bought for several reasons: its beauty, as a signal of prosperity and sophistication of the owner or as an investment that carries an expected monetary return. Extravagant art prices that are observed in rich countries give an indication of the existence of very high purchasing power that is channelled into the art market. Fashions and fades can drive the market for a while but, eventually, prices should converge to long-run values – the "prices of posterity" that thought Roger Fry.

Art prices are sensitive to macroeconomic and financial fluctuations, say cycles of expansion and contraction in the real economy and booms and busts in financial markets (ups and downs in asset prices). Average art price indices have behaved in a pro-cyclical way in the big recessions of the last 90 years (the Great Depression of the 1930s, stagflation of the 1970s, the global financial crisis in 2008–2009). In contrast, in these episodes gold has been a counter-cyclical asset (a safe haven *per excellence*).

The art market is affected by physical indivisibilities, asymmetric information, significant transaction costs and liquidity issues affecting its efficiency. Nonetheless, and in spite of these intrinsic features, the recorded art market had global sales of U\$ 50 billion in 2020 down from near U\$ 65 billion in 2019 with the expectation that it will keep recover in coming years. In addition, techniques of collateralization and securitization are expanding the possibilities of acquiring art work to an increasing number of participants. Still, the art market is much smaller in volume than equity markets, real estate markets and currency markets.

Economic inequality with a high degree of wealth concentration at the top has promoted the segmentation and duality of the art market with sales concentrating in the upper end of the market dominated by a handful of big international galleries and auction houses. However, the medium and small-size galleries still account for near 80 percent of employment creation and number of sales in the art market. Money earned in finance, real estate, technology, retail, exploitation of natural resources and other activities is being channelled to acquire high-value art. In addition, private collectors have much more influence now in shaping the activities of public museums and other cultural organizations.

Geographically, the bulk of art market sales are concentrated in the United States of America, UK and China, with these three markets accounting for more than 80 percent of global art sales followed by France, Switzerland and Germany. The rise of the Chinese art market in the last two decades has been impressive and coincides with its new role rising as a global economic power.

New sophisticated financial mechanisms have been created to protect wealth and reduce taxation such as the use of freeports to store (tax-free), preserve, handle and trade artwork and luxuries.

This shows the opacity and lack of regulation of the high-end of the art market.

Public policy transformations in the art sector need to be directed to various fronts: first, to regulate the influence of big money to avoid that ownership of and enjoyment of art becomes only available to rich elites. Also to reduce the excessive influence of wealthy patrons in the board of directors of cultural institutions that need also a public presence. In this perspective, the state and civil society organizations need to re-assert their influence in the art sector through adequate government funding of public museums, the provision of income support mechanisms oriented to encourage emerging artists to continue their creative work and the financing of free-access exhibitions and other popular initiatives to make art available to the vast majority of the population. By shielding mainstream cultural institutions from an excessive dependence on private donors, they could have a more effective autonomy to include in their exhibitions overlooked experimentalist and innovative artists.

The *privatization of the art sector* is not uniform across countries. Advanced capitalist nations such as France, the United Kingdom, Germany, Spain, Scandinavian countries, the Netherlands and others mobilize substantial public resources in the funding of public museums and exhibitions making art reasonably accessible to the population interested in cultural affairs. In Latin American countries such as Mexico and, Argentina have a tradition of public support to culture and the arts and have mobilized considerable budgets directed to supporting public museums, exhibitions and helping promising artists and making sure art and culture is accessible to broad segments of the population. These countries hold leading public art collections and keep vibrant museums.

A second area is to advance in the *de-commodification* of the art sector (excessive influence of the profit motive in setting cultural priorities) by encouraging the autonomy of artistic collectives, the formation and consolidation of art cooperatives owned and managed by artists and art commons that are guided by motives different from obtaining monetary profits. This poses organizational and financial challenges not simple to handle in an era in which credit and financial instruments are geared to funding the most profitable sectors of the capitalist economy (finance, real estate, insurance, the upper-end segment of the art market). Money, logistic and organizational capacities are needed to support the middle and small-scale art sector and artists. A motivation of Keynes's idea for creating the Art Council in Great Britain in the 1940s was to ensure a *basic income for creative people* that would ensure their talents are allocated to creative endeavours liberating them, at least in part, of the necessity of making a living in other activities to support themselves and their family. The thinking was that solving the "economic problem" of the artists would enable them to devote their time and energies to produce art. This sympathetic and common-sense logic that artists and culture need to be supported is still very valid today.

Third, there is a need for revamping tax codes and set-up new, reasonable regulations in the art sector. A new institutional framework must promote fair taxation of high value art transactions at national and international levels earmarking the revenues so obtained to finance public museums, giving grants to artists and the teaching of art to children at schools and the youth in universities.

As segments of the art market are affected by secretive deals and manipulative practices, it is important to establish higher degrees of transparency in transactions taking place in auctions, galleries and informal sales. The compilation of a public database of sellers, buyers and prices at which artworks are sold would be an important step in that direction.

Another recommendation is the preparation of a *public registry of valuable art objects* at local, national and global levels that would be available to accountable public agencies holding a mandate to custody the cultural patrimony and heritage of countries. International cooperation to promote the public registry of art would be very valuable. As public resources for the art and culture tends to be scarce, the mobilization of co-funding from the private sector is needed to protect the art patrimony of cities and countries.

Protecting non-profit galleries, and individual artists and collectives from the pressures, dominance and exclusion of big galleries and auction houses would help employment generation in the art sector as smaller galleries create more jobs and would allow also a more pluralistic pool of artistic creators and agents, which could benefit historically marginalized communities in several manners.

Funding from international cooperation and the national state is important for supporting artists coming from poor slumps, rural communities, and underdeveloped countries. Finally, it is essential to shield in an intelligent way the art sector from the ups and downs of the business cycles, the effects of austerity policies, financial crises, global inequality and populist and xenophobic politics usually hostile to art and culture.

References

Adam, G. (2017) *The Dark Side of the Boom: The Excesses of the Art Market in the 21st Century*. UK: Lund Humphries, Ashgate Publishing.

Adam, G. (2014) *Big Bucks. The Explosion of the Art Market in the 21st Century*. UK: Lund Humphries, Ashgate Publishing.

Addison, T. (2008) "The International Mobility of Talent in the Cultural Sector" In A. Solimano, editor, *The International Mobility of Talent*, Oxford University Press.

Aubry, M., R. Kräussl, G. Manso and C. Spaenjers (2019) Machines and Masterpieces: Predicting Prices in the Art Auction Market. *Available at SSRN 3347175*.

Baumol (1986) "Unnatural value: Or art investment as floating crap game" *American Economic Review, AEA Papers and Proceedings*, 76, 10–14.

Bossier, M., C. Noe, M. Resch and L. Steiner (2014) "Art Collector Report 2014" Verlag für moderne Kunst Nürnberg GmbH, Nuremberg.

Burton, R., J. D. Jackson and R. D. Tollison (2017) *The Economics of the American Art. Issues, Artists and Institutions*, Oxford University Press.

Campbell, R. (2008) "Art as a financial investment" *The Journal of Alternative Investments*, Spring 10(4), 64–81.

Chambers, D., E. Dimson and C. Spaenjers (2017) "Art as an Asset: Evidence from Keynes the Collector", Mimeo.

Credit, Suisse (2017a) *Global Wealth Report* 2017, Research Institute.

Credit, Suisse (2017b) *Global Wealth Report Databook* 2017, Research Institute.

Cultural Heritage Resource (2009) About Cultural Heritage Resource. [online] Available at: https://web.stanford.edu/group/chr/drupal/ref/tax-deductible-property-donations-to-us-museums [Accessed August 24, 2018].

David, G. (2014) "Is Art Really a Safe-haven? Evidence from the French Market during World War I," CEB Working Paper #14/025. Centre Emile Durnheim. Universite Libre de Bruxelles.

David, G. and Oosterlinck, K. (2015) "War, Monetary Reform and the Belgian Art Market, 1945–1951" *Financial History Review*, 22 (2), 157–177.

De Marchi, N. and H. J. Van Miegroet (2006) *The History of Art Markets*, Chapter 3 in Handbook of the Economics of Art and Culture, Vol.1, pp.69–122, Elsevier.

Deloitte (2017) *Art and Finance Report* 2017, 5th Edition, Deloitte and ArTactic.

Ekelund, R. B., J. D. Jackson and R. Tollison (2017) *The Economics of American Art*, Oxford University Press.

Edwards, S. (2004) "The Economics of Latin American Art: Creativity Patterns and Rates of Return" *NBER Working Paper* 10302, from National Bureau of Economic Research, Inc. Cambridge.

Feliciano, H. (1995) *The Lost Museum. The Nazi Conspiracy to Steal the World's Greatest Work of Art*. New York: Basic Books.

Frazer, A. (2016) *In Museums, Money and Politics*, Massachusetts, MIT Press.

Freund, C. (2016) Rich People, Poor Countries. The Rise of Emerging Markets Tycoons and their Mega Firms, Washington DC, Peterson Institute of International Economics.

Fry, R. (1926) *Art and Commerce*. London: Hogarth Press.

Fry, R. (1909[1920]) "An Essay in Aesthetics", 1909, in *New Quarterly*, reprinted in Vision and Design, 1920, London: Chatto and Windus Ltd.

Galenson, D. W. (2007) "Artists and the Market. From Leonardo and Titian to Andy Warhol and Damien Hirst" NBER WP, 13377.

Galenson, D. W. (2009) *Conceptual Revolutions in Twentieth-Century Art*, NBER Cambridge University Press, Cambridge UK and New York.

Goetzmann, W., L. Renneboog and C. Spaenjers (2011) "Art and Money", *American Economic Review*, 101 (3), pp.222–226.

Goodman, J. (2011) *Blooming in the Shadows: Unofficial Chinese Art, 1974–1985*. New York: China Institute.

Goodwin, C. D. (1999) *Art and the Market. Roger Fry on Commerce in Art*. Ann Arbour, MI: The University of Michigan Press.

Hicks, J. (1989) *A Market Theory of Money*, Oxford University Press.

Hiraki, T., A. Ito, D. A. Spieth and N. Take Ana (2009) "How did Japanese investment influence international art prices" *Journal of Financial and Quantitative Analysis*.

Horowitz, C. (2016) Who Should Pay for the Arts in America? The Atlantic.

Joy, A. and J. F Sherry (2004) "Framing considerations in the PRC: Creating value in the contemporary art market" *Consumption, Markets and Culture*, 7, 307–348.

Keynes, J. M. (1936. [1964]) *The General Theory of Employment, Interest and Money*. San Diego New York London: A Harvest/HBJ Book.

Kindleberger, Ch. P. (1978[2000]) Manias, Panics, and Crashes. A History of Financial Crises, Fourth Edition, Wiley Investment Classics, John Wiley & Sons, Inc. New York.

Korteweg, A., R. Kraussl and P. Werjijmeren (2016) "Does it pay to invest in art? A selection-corrected returns perspectives" *Review of Financial Studies*, 23, 3738–3772.

Kraeussl, R. and R. Logher (2010) "Emerging Art Markets", *Emerging Markets Review*, 11, pp. 301–318, Elsevier.

Kraeussl, R., T. Lehnert and N. Martelin (2016) "Is there a Bubble in the Art Market?" *Journal of Empirical Finance*, 35, 99–109, North Holland.

Lerer, M. and C. McGarriage (2018) "Art in the age of financial crises" *Visual Resources*, 34:1–2, 1–12. Taylor & Francis, Online.

Mandel, B. R. (2009) "Art as an investment and conspicuous consumption good" *American Economic Review*, 99, 1653–1663.

McAndrew, C. (2018) *The Art Market 2018*, Art Basel & UBS Report.

McAndrew, C. (2019) *The Art Market 2019*, Art Basel & UBS Report.

Mei, J. and M. Moses (2002) "Art as investment and the underperformance of masterpieces: Evidence from 1875–2002" *American Economic Review*, 92, 1656–1668.

Minsky, H. P. (1975) *John Maynard Keynes*, McGraw Hill.

Minsky, H. P. (1982) *Can "It" Happen Again. Essays on Instability and Finance*. New York: M.E. Sharpe, Inc. Armonk.

Minsky, H. P. (1986) *Stabilizing an Unstable Economy*, McGraw Hill.

Modern Art in China, Facts and Details. www.factsanddetails.com.

Nicholas, L. H. (1995) *The Rape of Europe. The Fate of Europe's Treasures in the Third Reich and Second World War*. New York: Vintage Books.

Oosterlinck, K. (2011) "The Price of Degenerate Art" *CEB Working Paper 09/031*, Brussels.

Perry, J. (1994) "Shanghai's strike wave of 1957" *The China Quarterly*, 137, 1–27.

Rezaee, A. and I. Sequeira (2018) "How Art Market Reacts to Financial Crises". Available at SSRN: https://SSRN.com/abstract=3167739.

Renneboog, L. and C. Spaenjers (2013) "Buying beauty: On prices and returns in the art market" *Management Science*, 59, 36–53.

Renda, A. (2015) "A History of the Art Market: From 15th Century Florence to Sotheby's-E Bay Agreement", *LUISS Guido Carli*, Libera Internazionale Universita Degli Studi Sociale.

Robertson, I. and D. Chong (Eds) (2008) *The Art Business*. London and New York: Routledge.

Rosen, S. (1981) "The economics of superstars" *The American Economic Review*, 71(5), 845–858.

Rosenberg, H. (1967) "Collective, Ideological, Combative" In T. B. Hess and J. Ashbery, (Eds), *Avant Garde Art*. New York, p. 88.

Russian Avant Garde (1981) *The George Costakis Collection*. New York: Harry, N. Abrams Inc. Publishers.

Secrest, M. (2005) *Duveen: A Life in Art*, The University of Chicago Press.

Solimano, A. (1991) "The Economies of Central and Eastern Europe: An Historical and International Perspective", chapter 2 in Corbo, V., Coricelli, F. And J. Bossask, editors, Reforming Central and Eastern European Economies. Initial Results and Challenges, A World Bank Symposium, The World Bank, Washington DC.

Solimano, A. (2010) *International Migration, Crisis and Globalization*, Cambridge University Press.

Solimano, A. (2014) *Economic Elites, Crises and Democracy*. Oxford University Press.

Solimano, A. (2017) *Global Capitalism in Disarray. Debt, Inequality and Austerity*. Oxford University Press.

Solimano, A. (2018a) "Wealth Mobility: Implications for Inequality" *Research & Publications*, DOC-RI, February, Berlin.

Solimano, A. (2018b) "Global Mobility of the Wealthy and their Assets: An Overview" *Investment Migration Council, Research Paper* 2018/02.

Solimano, A. (2018c) "Crypto-currencies, Speculation and the Evolution of Monetary Systems" Working Paper, International Center for Globalization and Development, CIGLOB.

Solimano, A. (2020) *A History of Big Recessions in the Long Twentieth Century*, Cambridge University.

Solimano, A. (Ed) (2008) *The International Mobility of Talent*. Oxford University Press.

Solimano, A. and P. Solimano (2020) "Global Capitalism, Wealth Inequality and the Art Market" In Hamed Hosseini (Ed), *Handbook of Transformative Global Studies*, Routledge: London and New York.

Sarabianov, D. V. and N. L Adaskina (1990) *Popova*. New York: Harry N. Abrams Inc. Publishers.

State Russian Museum (2000) *Malevich's Circle*. Moscow: Palace Editions.

Taylor, L. (2020) *Macroeconomic Inequality from Reagan to Trump*, Cambridge University Press (with contributions from Ozlem Omer).

Tingyou, C. (2003) *Chinese Calligraphy*, China Intercontinental Press.

Veblen, T. (1899[1994]) *The Theory of the Leisure Class*, Dover Thrift. Editions. www.doverpublications.com.

Want, A. (2014/4) "Apolitical Art, Private Experience and Alternative Subjectivity in China's Cultural Revolution" *China Perspectives* (Online), OpenJournals.

Worthington, A. C. and H. Higgs (2004) "Art as an investment: Risk, return and portfolio diversification in major painting markets" *Accounting & Finance*, 44(2), 257–271.

(Zenya) National Wan, Kwan (2017) "China's Demand in Works of Art and Six Typologies of Chinese Collectors in Four Groups", Haute Ecole de Gestion de Geneva.

Index

Italicized and **bold** pages refer to figures and tables respectively, and page
numbers followed by "n" refer to footnotes.

abstract expressionism 17, 19, 42, 86
Alandia Pantoja, Miguel 15
Alberti, Leon Battista 42
Alighieri, Dante 11
American hegemony 17, 21–22, 85
American Modernism 11
Argentina 89
Armory Show of 1913 11
art: collateralization 38, 87;
    collection 44; defining 39–40;
    degenerate 18; digital 2, 42; funds
    38, 46n12, 66–67, 90; investments
    3, 51, 63, 68; securitization 38, 43,
    87, 88
art centres 85; New York 17–18;
    Paris 9–10
artistic creativity 13, 40–42, 61, 86
"artists of the left" 13
art market 88; anatomy of 37–38;
    authentication costs 46, 48;
    concentration and polarization
    52–55; COVID-19 impact on 21;
    East Asian 22; economic val-
    uation 45–48; evolution of 85;
    features of 43–55, **55**; financial
    experts 38; financialization and
    globalization of 50–52; illegal
    activities 49–50, 50n17; impact
    of wars 61, 85; indivisibility
    and heterogeneity 43–44;
    lemons problem 48; liquidity
    45–48; online 38; recessions

and 58; vs. stock and property
    markets **55**; stock market
    crashes 57–58; transaction costs
    48–49; value at posterity 47;
    winners-take-all-market 54; see
    also demand; supply of artwork
art prices 87–88; assessing and pre-
    dicting 43–44; average 77, 77, 88;
    in China 34; correlations 81, 82,
    83, 84; equity prices vs. 58; extrav-
    agant levels 2–3, 53; fundamental
    value 2, 48, 87; gold prices vs. 77,
    77, 82; hyperinflation 57; macro-
    economic cycles and 59–60; rise
    of 66; stock prices vs. 58, 76, **76**;
    in US, UK and France 77–78, 78;
    volatility in 78, **79**; in World War I
    and World War II 61–64
art schools 27, 42
art theft 18, 49, 61
ashcan school 11
auction houses: in China 23;
    Christie's 11, 25, 33, 34; Phillips de
    Pury & Company 11, 33; Sotheby's
    10–11, 25, 33, 34
Auction of Cultural Relics 22–23
auctions: in China 34; Dutch system
    9; English system 9; segment 54
authentication costs 46, 48

barter economies 46, 46n14
Bell, Clive 40

blockchain technologies 48, 87
Bolshevik revolution 4, 12
Botticelli, Sandro 11
Breton, Andre 15, 16
Brigadas Ramona Parra (BRP) 15
Bruges 8–9
brush painting 28

calligraphy 26–27
Campbell, R. 51
Cao-Cao She (Green society) 31–32
capitalism 40, 56, 85; global 4, 69, 87;
    managed 20; neoliberal 20–21
capitalist elites 65
Castelli, Leo 20
Central Academy of Fine Arts of
    Beijing 29
Chagall, Marc 12
Chile, muralism in 4, 15
China 75n2; Auction of
    Cultural Relics 22–23; wealth
    concentration 70
China Guardian 33, 34
China National Gallery of Art 30, 31
Chinese Artists' Association (CAA)
    29
Chinese art market 22–23, 33–35, 88
Chinese art sector 5–6; art and
    revolution 24, 29–30; art schools
    27; Cao-Cao She group 31–32;
    cultural revolution 24, 25, 30;
    demand 34–35; exhibitions 28;
    Japan's cultural influence 28;
    Maoist period 24, 29–30; polit-
    ical pop 32; post-Mao period
    25, 30–33; socialist realism 25;
    traditional 5, 26–28; Western
    influences 27–28; Wuming group
    30–31; XingXing group 31
Christie's 11, 25, 33, 34
civilization 40
Clark, Kenneth 40
Coase, Ronald 48
collateralization 38, 87, 88
commodification 5, 87; see also
    de-commodification
complex monetary economy 46
conceptual innovators 41
constructivism 12
Costakis, George 13

COVID-19 pandemic: economic
    crisis 21; gold prices 52
creativity 13, 40–42, 61, 86
cultural revolution 24, 25, 30

David, G. 62, 64
da Vinci, Leonardo 42; "Salvatori
    Mundi" 2, 53
de-commodification 89; see also
    commodification
degenerate art 18
demand 3, 37; as aesthetic consump-
    tion 45; changes in 45; for Chinese
    art 34–35; effective 45; Fry's
    typology 39
Detroit Industry Murals 14
digital art 42; *Everydays: the first
    5,000 days* 2
donations 67–68; see also fundings
Durand-Ruel, Paul 10
Duveen, Joseph 10

economic elites 4–5, 21, 35, 65
economic globalization 4, 21
economic valuation of art 45–48; see
    also art prices
Edme -Francois Gersaint 9
El Primer Gol de Chile (the first goal
    of the Chilean people) 15
Estenssoro, Victor Paz 15
Everydays: the first 5,000 days 2
exhibitions 13, 28, 89
experimentalist innovators 41

faking 49
Federal Art Project (FAP) 17
financial crises 5; COVID-19 and 21;
    see also recession
financialization 5, 50–52, 87
financial repression 19, 85
Florence 8
forgery 49, 50n17
France 8; art prices in 77–78, *78*;
    wealth's share of the top 1 percent
    71n9
Franco, Francisco 15
freeports 68–69
Frel, Jiri 68n5
French art 11
Freud, Sigmund 16

Fry, Roger 39, 40, 47, 88
fundamental value 2, 48, 87
fundings 38, 46n12, 66–67, 90

Galenson, D. W. 10n3, 41
Garcia Meza, Luis 15
*General Theory of Employment,
Interest and Money* (Keynes) 47
genius 40–42
Germany, art theft and looting 18,
50, 86
global art market *23*; value and
volume of transactions **59**, *60*
global art price indices 75–76, **76**,
81–84
global capitalism 4, 69, 87
global financial crisis (2008–2009)
vs. gold prices **80**, 81
globalization 4, 21, 50–52
Goering, Hermann 18
Goetzmann, W. 58
gold prices: art prices *vs.* 77, **77**,
82; COVID-19 crises 52; global
financial crisis of 2008–2009 **80**,
81; Great Depression of 1930s **80**,
80–81; stagflation of the 1970s **80**,
81; stock market prices *vs.* 81, *82*
Gorky, Arshile 19
Great Depression of 1930s 58; gold
prices **80**, 80–81
Great Leap Forward 30
gross financial return 51
"group of eight" event 11
Guernica 14–15
Guggenheim, Peggy 20
Gutt, Camille 64n10

Haystacks [Monet series] 2, 53
hedge funds 38
hedonic regression (HR) method
43–44
Hicks, John 46
Hirst, Damien 42
Hockney, David 2, 3
homo-economicus 42
Hong Kong art market 22, 23
hyperinflation 53, 57

illegal activities 49–50, 50n17
Imana Pantoja, Gil 15

Impressionism 41
inequality 33, 88; wealth 6, 70–72
ink paintings 27, 28
innovation 12, 41, 87
intellectual painting 28
intelligentsia 37
investments 3, 51, 63, 68

Japan: art market 22; cultural
influence on China 28
Jeu de Paume museum 18
Jewish art 18

Kahlo, Frida 15
Kandinsky, Wassily 12
Keynes, John Maynard 39, 40; art
collection 44; Art Council in
Great Britain 89–90; effective
demand 45; *General Theory of
Employment, Interest and Money*
47; marginal efficiency of capital
47; motives for holding money 46
Khrushchev, Nikita, "revisionist"
model 25
Kline, Franz 19
Kooning, Willem de 19
Koons, Jeff 2, 3, 42
Kraeussl, R. 51

Lehnert, T. 51
lemons problem 48
Lenin, Vladimir Ilyich 14
liquidity 45–48
Lissitzky, El 12–13
literati painting (intellectual
painting) 28
Luks, George 11

Macbeth Gallery 11
machine learning method 44
macroeconomic cycles 59–60
Malevich, Kazimir 12
managed capitalism 20
"Man at the Crossroads" mural 14
Mandel, B. R. 51
Maoist China 24, 29–30
Mao Zedong [Mao Tse Tung] 4,
24, 25; idol of 31; One-hundred
Flowers Campaign 29–30; Talks
at Yunnan Forum on Literature

and Art 29; Warhol's portrayal of 32, 32n8
marginal efficiency of capital 47
Martelin, N. 51
mass of ignorant people 47
Matta, Roberto 4, 15, 17, 19
Mellon, Andrew 17
Mexican revolution of 1910 4, 13–14
Mexico, muralism in 4, 14–16, 37, 86
Minsky, Hyman 46, 47
Modern art 1, 3, 10n3, 22
modernists 11
Modotti, Tina 15
monetary reform 64
monetary valuation of art 45–48
Monet, Claude 10n3, 43; Haystacks 2, 53
money overhang 64n12
Motherwell, Robert 19
murals/muralism 4; in Chile 15; Detroit Industry 14; Guernica 14–15; Man at the Crossroads 14; in Mexico 14–16, 86; Picasso and 14–15; Rivera and 14; and social transformation 15
Museum of Modern Art in New York (MOMA) 19, 67
Museums, Money, and Politics (2016) (Fraser) 67

National Gallery of Art 17
Nazis, art looting 18, 50, 86
neoclassic theory 45
neoliberal capitalism 20–21
New York, as art centre 17–18
Nixon, Richard 32
non-fungible tokens (NTF) 48–49, 87
not-for-profit art organizations 36
"nouveaux riches" 18, 63

oil painting 27
O'Keeffe, Georgia 11
One-hundred Flowers Campaign 29–30
Oosterlinck, K. 64
Orozco, Jose Clemente 14, 17

Pareto, Wilfredo 46n14
Paris, as art centre 9–10, 85
Paris Salon 9–10

Phillips de Pury & Company 11, 33
Picasso, Pablo 4; Guernica 14–15
Plato 39
polarization 52–55
political pop 32
Pollock, Jackson 17, 19, 43
Poly Auction 33
Poly Group 33
pop art 42, 86
Popova, Liubov 12
Portrait of an Artist (Pool with Two Figures) 3
post-Mao's China 6, 25, 30–33
"The Price of Degenerate Art" (Oosterlinck) 63
primary art markets 8
private collectors 66, 88
private funding 66
privatization 66, 89
property markets 55
psychic return 51
public funding 66, 67
public policy 39, 89
public registry 90

Qi Baishi 28n3
Qiu Deshu 32

Rabbit (Koons) 3
recession 57–58, 72–73; and art market 58; origin of 58
Renaissance ideal 8, 42
repeated sales regression (RSR) method 43–44
revolution, art and 11–14; in China 24, 29–30; conceptual 86
riggatieri 9
Rivera, Diego 14
Rodchenko, Alexander 12
Rosenberg, Harold 13
Rosen, S. 54n25
Rothko, Mark 19
Russian avant-garde 11–13

safe haven asset/investment 5, 51–52
Salvatori Mundi 2, 53
search costs 46
secondary art markets 8
securitization 38, 43, 87, 88
Shanghai Municipal Art Gallery 28

Shinn, Everett 11
Siqueiros, David Alfaro 14, 17
Sloan, John 11
socialist realism 25, 29
Solon Romero, Walter 15
Sotheby's 10–11, 25, 33, 34
spot market value 47
stagflation of the 1970s, gold prices
  80, 81
Stieglitz, Alfred 11
stock markets **55**; crashes and art
  markets 57–58
stock prices 75n2; art prices *vs.* 58,
  76, **76**; gold prices *vs.* 81, *82*
stolen art 5; *see also* art theft
Sundaresan, Vignesh [aka
  Metakovan] 2
super-rich 69–73
supply of artwork 36, 45
surrealism 15, 16, 86

Tamayo, Rufino 16
taxation 68, 90
technology 48, 87
tokenization 48–49
Tolstoy, Leon 39
traditional Chinese art 5, 26–28
transaction costs 5, 48

United Kingdom: art prices in
  77–78, *78*; wealth's share of the top
  1 percent 71n9
United States: abstract expressionism in 17, 19, 42, 86; art investment
  funds 46n12; art prices in 77–78,
  78; economic depression 16–17;
  Federal Art Project 17; New Deal

37; NYC as art centre 17–18;
  wealth concentration 70; wealth's
  share of the top 1 percent 71n9;
  World War II 17–18

Vaca, Lorgio 15
valuation of artwork 45–48
value at posterity 47
Van Gogh, Vincent 47
volatility 78, **79**

Wang Keping 31
Warhol, Andy 42, 43; Mao portraits
  32, 32n8
wars 56, 60; impact on art prices
  61–64
wealth concentration 69–70, *70*, **71**,
  72, 73, 88
wealth effect 72
wealth inequality 6, 70–72, 88
Western art 24, 25; Chinese demand
  for 34
What is Art (Tolstoy) 39
Wilde, Oscar 45
Winkelmann, Mike [aka Beeple] 2,
  49
Wolf, Virginia 39
World War I 4, 11, 46, 86; art prices
  in 61–64
World War II 4, 17–18, 50, 85; art
  prices in 61–64
written painting 28
Wuming (no name) Painting Group
  30–31

XingXing (star-star) Painting
  Society 31

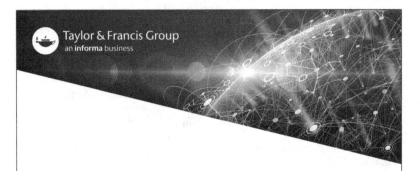

Taylor & Francis eBooks

www.taylorfrancis.com

A single destination for eBooks from Taylor & Francis
with increased functionality and an improved user
experience to meet the needs of our customers.

90,000+ eBooks of award-winning academic content in
Humanities, Social Science, Science, Technology, Engineering,
and Medical written by a global network of editors and authors.

TAYLOR & FRANCIS EBOOKS OFFERS:

A streamlined
experience for
our library
customers

A single point
of discovery
for all of our
eBook content

Improved
search and
discovery of
content at both
book and
chapter level

REQUEST A FREE TRIAL
support@taylorfrancis.com

Printed in the United States
by Baker & Taylor Publisher Services

Printed in the United States
by Baker & Taylor Publisher Services